ALL YOU NEED TO KNOW ABOUT THE BIBLE

Book 3:
have we got the right books?

BRIAN H EDWARDS

DayOne

© Day One Publications 2017

ISBN 978-1-84625-586-1

All Scripture quotations, unless stated otherwise, are from The Holy Bible, New International Version Copyright © 1973, 1978, 1984 International Bible Society

British Library Cataloguing in Publication Data available

Published by Day One Publications
Ryelands Road, Leominster, HR6 8NZ
Telephone 01568 613 740   Fax 01568 611 473
North America Toll Free 888 329 6630
email—sales@dayone.co.uk
web site—www.dayone.co.uk

Cover design by Kathryn Chedgzoy
Printed by T J International

ALL YOU NEED TO KNOW ABOUT THE BIBLE

BRIAN H EDWARDS

Book 3
Have we got
the right books?

The series outline

Book 1 Can we trust it?
What this book is all about

1. What's the Bible all about?
The Master Plan with Jesus Christ as the theme

2. Remarkable prophecy
What do we do with these incredible predictions?

3. Evidence of an eyewitness
Proof that the writers were there

4. Did Jesus really live?
Jesus fixed in history

5. Living letters for living churches
Marks of real letters to real Christians

6. Fact or fiction?
Evidence of the Old Testament written in its time

Book 2 Big claims from a unique book

1. The God who reveals himself
Evidence everywhere

2. Ultimate truth
God-given and without error

3. Jesus and his Bible
What Scriptures did Jesus use?

4. The apostles and their Bible
What Scriptures did the apostles use?

5. Absolute authority
Big claims by prophets, Jesus, and apostles

6. Is the Bible enough?
Sufficient and final

7. The Chicago statement
The inerrancy statement of the International Council for Biblical Inerrancy

Book 3 Have we got the right books?

1. Who thought of a Bible?
The idea of a collection of books

2. The Jews and their Bible
The books in the Old Testament

3. The early Christians and their Bible
The beginning of a New Testament

4. A growing collection
The development of the accepted books

5. A complete New Testament
The books accepted across the Christian world

6. Who wrote the books?
The writers of the New Testament books

7. Helpful letters not in the Bible
More instructions for the young churches

8. A library of lies
The writings of the heretics

Appendix
A chart of the church Fathers

Book 4 A journey from then to now

1. From flames to fame
The story of the English Bible

2. How old is the Old Testament?
The earliest copies

3. How old is the New Testament?
The earliest copies

4. Discovering the best text
Why are some verses different?

5. Which translation?
The dilemma of many versions

Book 5 Sense as well as faith

1. Tearing the Bible apart
The Bible and its critics

2. Great minds on a great book
What scholars say

3. Digging up the evidence
Archaeology confirms the truth

4. Guidelines for combat
Errors and contradictions?

5. Solving the problems
Resolving some of the issues

Book 6 Enjoy your Bible!

1. It's for you, it's alive—read it!
The best way to read the Bible

2. Reading the Bible with common sense
A guide to a good understanding

3. A bit more common sense
Types, symbols and dangers to avoid

4. Getting to grips with the Old Testament
A chart of the books in their proper place

5. Piecing the Gospels together
A harmony of the life of Jesus

6. Where did they write their letters?
The Acts of the Apostles and where all the letters fit in

7. Reading the Bible from cover to cover
A careful plan to read it all in eighteen months!

8. Take time with God
Spending time each day with God

Contents

What this book is all about

If the Bible really is what it claims to be—the final and authoritative revelation from God—it is essential that we should be certain that in the sixty-six books that make up its pages we have exactly the ones God intended to be there, no more and no less. And if there were forty writers over a period of fifteen hundred years, can we possibly know who they all were?

It's common today to suggest that we have all the wrong books in the Bible or that it was a mere lottery which ones eventually entered the 'canon'. In this third book in the series we examine the question of how the collection of books came into existence; a collection that would be divine in its authorship, fixed in its number, and final in its authority.

We begin with the Jews and their Bible. This is the easy part, because there was never any serious disagreement among the Jews about which books belonged in their Hebrew Scriptures and which should be rejected. The Jewish 'Bible' is exactly the same as our Old Testament. They numbered and arranged the books differently, but the same books are there, and no others. Chapter 2 examines the growth of the collected books of our Bible, and why the *Apocrypha* was never part of this.

Because the Jews believed that God had given them their Scriptures as a record of the history of their nation, and much else besides, it would be natural for the early Christians to expect the life of their Lord and Saviour to be recorded as well. All the evidence points to the completion of the four Gospels long before the end of the first century. In addition, the letters of the apostles were eagerly read, copied, and shared among the churches. Slowly, as the various books were gathered together, a New Testament 'canon', or collection, was formed. Significantly, although the early church leaders after the apostles quoted frequently and extensively from the letters of the apostles, they always made it clear that these alone, unlike their own writing, carried divine authority.

Could some of the twenty-seven books in the New Testament have been written by anyone other than those names that are either traditionally given to them, or are actually there in the greetings? The evidence in most cases is overwhelmingly simple. Unfortunately, critical minds that refuse to accept the plain evidence are reluctant to let go their theories. For this reason, chapter 6 of this book considers the evidence for the authorship of each of the New Testament books.

Those early church leaders after the time of the apostles, were also writing to the young Christian churches. Many wrote encouraging and challenging letters: like Clement of Rome who had to re-run some of the problems Paul faced in his own letters to the Christians at Corinth. Ignatius of Antioch wrote seven warm pastoral letters to various churches on his way to martyrdom in Rome. For his part, Irenaeus of Lyons penned a mammoth five volume rebuttal of heretical views to guard the churches against error. Not all Christians today will have time to read the voluminous writing of these early Christian leaders, so in chapter 7 there is an overview of the quality of their writing.

By contrast, under the heading 'A library of lies', some of the unorthodox writing from the literature known as 'pseudepigrapha' is introduced. A little knowledge of this material, which is often bizarre and always heretical, is sufficient to show how valuable by contrast are the Gospels and letters of the apostles. To know something of the heretical Gnostics and others, and their foolish attempts to supplement the biblical Scriptures, is to be armed against the criticisms of those who try to undermine the true books of the New Testament. Much of it is the 'hollow and deceptive philosophy' (Colossians 2:8) that Paul refers to.

By the close of the fourth century, Christianity had been established under the Emperor Constantine as the official religion of the Roman Empire. This was tarnished by the slow growth of the church in Rome wielding an unspiritual power across Western Europe. This resulted in the Bible becoming a closed book to anyone except those who had the ability and authority to read the Latin translation. A Bible in English was unknown for the next one thousand years and when it was, the fires of martyrdom began. This is where the fourth book in this series begins.

1. Who thought of a Bible?

The early disciples of Jesus were schooled in the importance of the Hebrew Scriptures (our Old Testament) and it is only to be expected that they would want the life and teaching of Jesus to be written down.

The idea of a canon

Whilst pagan religions vaguely share with Judaism and Christianity the idea of 'inspiration' for their sacred texts, nothing in the ancient world religions compares with the clear Judaeo-Christian concept of a collection of authoritative books whose every word is considered to have a divine origin.

The word 'canon' comes from the Hebrew *kaneh* (a rod), and the Greek *kanon* (a reed). Among other things, the words referred equally to the measuring rod of the carpenter and the ruler of the scribe. It became a common word for anything that was the measure by which others were to be judged. In the ancient world, the Greek authors were referred to as the 'canon' for the 'absolute standard for pure language'.[1] Paul used the word twice in the New Testament, at 2 Corinthians 10:13 ('limits') and Galatians 6:16 ('rule') , though not in this context. However, the early church leaders used it to refer to the body of Christian doctrine accepted by the churches. Perhaps Clement of Alexandria, early in the third century, was the first to employ the word to refer to the Scriptures (the Old Testament).[2] Origen also used it in the same century,[3] and Athanasius a little later. From here on it became more common in Christian use with reference to a collection

---

1 B F Westcott, *The Canon of the New Testament*, p. 542.
2 Clement of Alexandria, *The Miscellanies*, Book VI.15. He comments, 'The ecclesiastical rule (canon) is the concord and harmony of the Law and the Prophets.'
3 Westcott, *The Canon of the New Testament*, p. 548 referring to Origen's commentary on Matthew 28: 'No one should use for the proof of doctrine books not included among the canonized Scriptures.'

of books that are fixed in their number, divine in their origin and universal in their authority.

The disciples of Jesus and the early Christian leaders would expect to have the life and teaching of Jesus in a written form. They were Jews, brought up to revere the Hebrew Scriptures as the very word of God; the written word was a vital part of their religion. To allow the life and teaching of Jesus to bounce around in oral chatter for decades whilst parchment, ink, pens and notebooks were ready to hand and all the disciples were capable of writing, is surely too much to expect of the first Christians. See Book 1 chapter 3 in this series for reading and writing in the first century.

The thirteen letters of Paul, which as we will see were all accepted by the churches from the earliest times, assume the existence of the Gospels. Paul's quotation from Luke 10:7 in 1 Timothy 5:18 is evidence of his awareness of the Gospel. Therefore, Paul had no need to authenticate the life of Christ. Paul accepts the nativity of Jesus, his life and crucifixion, and the resurrection as well known by his readers and can go directly to the theological significance of each. If the Gospels were not available, it is hard to imagine why Paul would not have defended the historical reality of the life of Jesus in more detail. Even in his defence of the literal resurrection of Jesus in 1 Corinthians 15, Paul focuses only briefly on the detail and is anxious to explain its implication.

The battle for the canon

The battle being fought today is age old. The existence of the documents that are the subject of so much public interest is not new. The *Nag Hammadi Library* (see chapter 8) is a collection of Gnostic books that early church leaders were exposing well before the close of the second century. The *Gospel of Judas* is of interest only because at last we have a copy of it; its existence has been known since the Christian leader Irenaeus wrote against it more than nineteen hundred years ago. The attraction of these ancient documents lies in their strange and esoteric twist of the truth and their opposition to the New Testament texts.

One hundred and thirty years ago, B Harris Cowper translated a number of the false gospels and letters available at that time and confessed: 'Before I undertook this work I never realised, so completely as I do now, the impassable character of the gulf which separates the genuine Gospels from these.' Cowper concluded, 'They are of no historical or doctrinal authority, and were never officially recognised in the Church.'[4]

Cowper quoted the severe judgment of the nineteenth century scholar, Bishop Ellicott, writing some two decades earlier: 'From all alike—from orthodox fathers, from early historians, from popes, from councils, from Romanist divines and Protestant commentators—the same amount of contempt and reprobation had been expended on the Apocryphal Gospels, and yet they live and thrive, and are, perhaps, now as much and as curiously read as ever.'[5] A century and a half later, they are not only read but are being turned into popular novels for the diet of an unaware public.[6]

If only Peter, John and Paul had left us a list of books to be accepted for exclusive use by the church. However, in the middle of the nineteenth century, one of the most scholarly writers on this subject, Bishop Brooke Foss Westcott, a Fellow of Trinity College Cambridge, claimed, 'From the close of the second century the history of the Canon is simple and its proof clear.'[7] That may be overstated, but there are few who have studied the relevant documents more carefully or written more thoughtfully on the subject than the learned bishop.

Why did it take so long?

The autographs of the New Testament (the gospels and letters penned by the original writers) were written between AD 48 and 70 (John *may* have been a little later) and our first list of books (though incomplete) does not

---

4 B H Cowper, *The Apocryphal Gospels and other Documents Relating to the History of Christ* (Williams and Norgate, London and Edinburgh 1870), Preface and Introduction p. x.

5 Ellicott, *Cambridge Essays* 1856, p. 55.

6 For example: Irving Wallace in *The Word* (1972); Baigent, Leigh and Lincoln in *The Holy Blood and the Holy Grail* (1982); Gruber and Kersten in *The Original Jesus* (1995); Dan Brown *The Da Vinci Code* (2003).

7 B F Westcott, *The Canon of the New Testament During the First Four Centuries* (Macmillan & Co. Cambridge 1855), p. 8.

appear until AD 150 in the *Muratorian Canon*, and our first complete list in AD 240 by Origen of Alexandria. See chapter 4 for the details.

It is often assumed that the churches in the first century were a medley of conflicting and contrary beliefs with no authoritative scriptures to guide them. Irenaeus was leader of the church at Lyons in Gaul (France) around AD 180 and he had a fair appreciation of the church across the Roman empire at that time. Writing against the heresies of his day, Irenaeus expressed his conviction that there was a wide degree of unity and agreement among the churches:

'The Church, having received this preaching and this faith, although scattered throughout the whole world, yet, as if occupying but one house, carefully preserves it ... For the churches that have been planted in Germany do not believe or hand down anything different, nor do those of Spain, nor those in Gaul, nor those in Egypt, nor those in Libya, nor those which have been established in the central regions of the world ... Nor will any one of the rulers in the Churches, however highly gifted he may be in point of eloquence, teach doctrines different from these.'[8]

Similarly, Origen of Alexandria, writing only a few decades later than Irenaeus, whilst lamenting the presence of heretics so that

'many of those who profess to believe in Christ differ from each other, not only in small and trifling matters, but also on subjects of the highest importance, as for example regarding God, or the Lord Jesus Christ, or the Holy Spirit...' yet still he acknowledged a widespread acceptance of orthodox belief among the churches: 'the teaching of the Church, transmitted in orderly succession from the apostles, and remaining in the Churches to the present day, is still preserved, that alone is to be accepted as truth which differs in no respect from ecclesiastical and apostolical tradition.'[9]

That there were many who tried to stamp their own writings and their own brand of 'Christianity' upon the churches is unquestioned. So why the delay in a fixed list of canonical books?

---

8 Irenaeus *Against Heresies*, Book I, ch.10:2.
9 Origen, *De Principiis*, Preface 2.

COMMUNICATION WOULD HAVE BEEN SLOW TO SOME PARTS OF THE EMPIRE

By the time of the Edict of Milan in AD 313, by which the emperor Constantine legalised Christianity across the empire, there is evidence of churches already established in what we know today as Britain, France, Spain, North Africa (from Algiers and Tunisia across to Egypt and even down to Ethiopia), further east to Persia and back through Turkey and Greece to link with Italy. There is no reason to suppose that the church was not spilling well beyond these frontiers. It would have taken some time for any one church even to hear about all the apostolic Gospels and letters, let alone gather copies of them. A congregation at Antioch in Syria had first to hear that Paul had written to the church at Thessalonica—more than 800 miles and half a dozen provinces away—then they had to request a copy and wait for its arrival. And so on for all the twenty-seven books across all the churches.

NO SCROLL OR CODEX COULD EASILY CONTAIN MORE THAN ONE OR TWO BOOKS

It would be impossible to fit more than one Gospel onto a scroll, and even when codices (books) were used, the entire New Testament would be extremely bulky and very expensive to produce. It was therefore far more convenient for New Testament books to be copied singly or in small groups. The earliest complete New Testament in Greek measures over 40 by 35 cm (16 by 14 in).[10]

THE FIRST CENTURY CHRISTIANS EXPECTED THE IMMINENT RETURN OF CHRIST

The idea of a collection of books would not have occurred to all the churches, especially those that anticipated the return of Christ sooner rather than later.[11] They did not plan for the long-term future of the church. The early leaders were wholly ignorant of what might later

---

10 See Book 4 chapter 3 in this series for the available manuscripts.

11 William Barclay, and other more liberal scholars of the New Testament, claim that around AD 90 'There was a veritable epidemic of letter writing and something must have given it its impetus.' They provide the extremely unlikely theory that Paul's letters had been forgotten and were rediscovered! William Barclay, *The Making of the Bible*. (Lutterworth Press. London 1965), p. 68. A far more likely explanation is that the churches woke up to the reality that they were in for the long haul.

become debates over the content of the canon. For them it was evident that a writing from an apostle was a sufficient authority in itself.

ONLY WHEN THE HERETICS ATTACKED THE TRUTH WAS THE IMPORTANCE OF A CANON APPRECIATED

It was not until the mid-second century, when the Gnostics and other deviants began making their own selection of which books they considered authentic (and adding their own), that the orthodox leaders saw the necessity of stating which books had been recognised across the churches. See chapter 7.

NO ONE CHURCH OR LEADER CONTROLLED ALL THE OTHERS

Although there were strong and respected leaders among the churches, Christianity had no supremo bishop who dictated to all the others. After the death of the last apostle, each church was wholly independent and its bishop (leader) fiercely guarded that independence. When the church at Rome first began to throw its weight around, it was decidedly put in its place by the others.[12]

FOR TWO HUNDRED AND FIFTY YEARS, THE CHURCH WAS UNDER CONSTANT THREAT OF PERSECUTION

Until the edict of Milan in AD 313, persecution was at times severe. The emperor Decius set out to exterminate the church and demanded that all Christian books should be surrendered on pain of death. Paradoxically this both hindered and assisted the formation of a canon because the Christians were under siege and needed to know which texts could be surrendered to the authorities as 'non-canonical'.

THE EARLY LEADERS ASSUMED THE AUTHORITY OF THE GOSPELS AND THE APOSTLES

They did not see the necessity of repeatedly stating the obvious. They quoted from or alluded to the Gospels and apostles constantly in their

---

12 Irenaeus in *Against Heresies*, Book III, Ch. 3:2, certainly referred to Rome as a leading church, but he made it clear that he was using it merely as an example because it was so well known and 'it would be very tedious … to reckon up the successions of all the Churches.'

writings, and that was apparently sufficient for the churches. They no more felt it necessary to keep on insisting on the exclusive authority and divine authorship of the Gospels and apostles than a modern-day writer or preacher does.

In the light of all this, it is remarkable that by AD 150 the *Muratorian Canon*, as we shall see, can provide a list close to the one we are familiar with today.

Centuries before the Council of Florence (1439–1443) finally settled the limits of the New Testament canon for the church of Rome, the issue had been settled and all that remained were scattered sections of the church, the deviant cults, and occasional individuals here and there who added or doubted the odd book or two. To claim that this meant that the canon was still in a state of flux in the fifteenth century would be like saying that because the Mormons today add *The Book of Mormon*, *The Pearl of Great Price* and *The Doctrines and Covenants* to the twenty-seven book of the New Testament, then the canon is still not fixed in the twenty-first century.

What decided which books should be in the Bible?

At first the churches had no need to define what made a book special and equal to the Old Testament Scriptures. If the letter came from Paul or Peter, that was sufficient. However, it was not long before others began writing additional letters and gospels either to fill the gaps or to propagate their own ideas (see chapter 8). Some tests became necessary and over the course of the next two hundred years five were used at one time or another.

APOSTOLIC—DOES IT COME FROM AN APOSTLE?

The first Christians looked for apostolic authority, just as the Jews had expected their Scriptures to be from the prophets. If the authorship of the books was unimportant, Paul would not have been insistent that his readers should be reassured that the letters they received came from his pen (1 Corinthians 16:21; Galatians 6:11; Colossians 4:18; 2 Thessalonians 3:17; Philemon 19). The heretics were apparently eager to send out their own writings under an apostolic name (2 Thessalonians 2:2).

Not only were the New Testament writers confident of their own divine authority (1 Thessalonians 2:13), but they accorded the same to each other (2 Peter 3:16). The test for fellowship was obedience to apostolic authority (2 Thessalonians 3:14).

In AD 180 Irenaeus, bishop of Lyons, posed the question: 'How should it be if the apostles themselves had not left us writings?'[13] His first test was that they should be written either by an apostle or by men closely associated with an apostle. Papias was eager to establish Paul behind Luke's Gospel and Peter behind Mark's; similarly, Origen might doubt that Paul was the author of Hebrews, but thought Luke, Paul's travelling companion, probably was. The *Muratorian Canon* rejected the *Shepherd of Hermas*, (see chapters 4 and 7), because it was 'after the time' of the apostles.

In the second century, Tertullian recorded a deacon in an Asian church being severely disciplined for writing the pseudo *Acts of Paul* under the apostle's name. Without doubt, the written word of an apostle was not merely a means by which people would be led into the truth, it was the truth; it was the basis of faith and the authority for it.

ANCIENT—HAS IT BEEN USED FROM THE EARLIEST TIMES?

If a book was clearly apostolic by its authorship, then it must have been available from the earliest days of the Christian church. When the compiler of the *Muratorian Canon* expressed his interest in the *Shepherd of Hermas*, he also recognised that it could not be numbered among the accepted books because it was too late in its composition. The *Acts of Paul* was one of the earliest pieces of non-canonical writing and is not especially unhelpful in its content, but because it was compiled sometime around the mid-second century, and its author was known to be a deacon in Asia, it was never considered among the canonical books.

Early in the fourth century, Athanasius listed the New Testament canon as we know it today and claimed that these were the books 'received by us through tradition as belonging to the Canon'.[14] At the end of that century,

---

13 Irenaeus, *Against Heresies*, Book III, Ch. 4:1.
14 Athanasius, *Festal Epistle*, XXXIX.

the Council meeting at Carthage in AD 397 listed the twenty-seven books of the canon, adding that they are 'what we have received from our fathers.'

ACCURATE—DOES IT CONFORM TO THE ACCEPTED TEACHING OF THE CHURCHES?

As we have seen from Irenaeus and Origen, there was widespread agreement among the churches across the empire on the content of the Christian message. Irenaeus asked the question whether a particular writing was consistent with what the churches taught. This immediately ruled out the Gnostic material.

Most of the false writings betrayed themselves at this point. Serapion, the leader at Antioch from AD 200–210, was attracted to the *Gospel of Peter* until, on closer inspection, he realised that it contained hints of heresy. The *Gospel of Peter*, the *Acts of Peter* and the *Apocalypse of Peter* were excluded from all canons because they did not contain apostolic theology.

Liberal critics, over the last one hundred and fifty years, have little interest in correct theology and therefore the canon can be wide open. This was certainly not so for the apostles and their successors. The faith 'once for all entrusted to the saints' (Jude 3), was vital for the health of the churches and for this, an authoritative body of books that contained the truth was vital. Without a secure canon, there could be no certain theology.

ACCEPTED—ARE MOST OF THE CHURCHES USING IT?

Naturally it took time for letters to circulate among the churches and some, like the Gospels, would probably travel more rapidly than others. Some of the letters of Paul dealt with local issues that another church may not have seen as relevant to their situation. However, the great majority of the New Testament books, some twenty-three of the twenty-seven, were almost universally accepted well before the middle of the second century, as the *Muratorian Canon* witnesses.

When Justin Martyr, (mid-second century), informed the emperor of the typical Christian Sunday worship meeting, he added, in such a casual way that it was assumed to be understood as a collected body of books, that they read the 'memoirs of the apostles or the writings of the prophets.' Both Origen, (mid-third century), and Eusebius, (early fourth century), claimed to present a list of the books accepted 'throughout the churches'. The four Gospels, for example, were for Origen 'the only indisputable ones in the church of God under heaven.' For his part, Eusebius began his lists with the twenty-two books that were universally accepted by the churches. This was also the position of both Jerome and Augustine in the early fifth century.

When tradition carries the weight of the overwhelming majority of churches throughout the widely scattered Christian communities across the vast Roman Empire, with no one church controlling the beliefs of all the others, it must be taken seriously.

AUTHENTIC—DOES IT HAVE THE RING OF TRUTH?

The authoritative voice of the prophets 'This is what the Lord says', is matched by the apostles' claim to write, not the words of men, but the words of God (1 Thessalonians 2:13). Does the book have that 'ring of truth' that sets it apart from other literature?

The church leaders recognised the voice of the Spirit in the books that formed the accepted canon. Origen wrote of the Scriptures breathing 'the Spirit of fullness' and added that there is nothing 'whether in the Law or in the Prophets, in the Evangelists [the Gospels] or in the Apostles, which does not descend from the fullness of the Divine Majesty.'[15] Clement of Rome believed that Paul wrote 'under the inspiration of the Spirit.' Even when these leaders themselves wrote to the churches and believed they were led by the Spirit, they were careful always to distance themselves from the unique authority of the apostles in the Scriptures.

The unity of the New Testament books was, and always has been, a remarkable phenomenon. Certainly, the leaders of the churches in the first three centuries recognised the books that 'belonged' together and those that, even though they may be useful, were of an altogether different family.

Not one of these five tests may be sufficient in itself. However, it was the cumulative evidence of all five, not least the first, that led to the steady strength of the books that eventually settled into the recognised canon.

---

15 Origen, *Homilies on Joshua*, XX.

Chapter 1

DIVINE PROVIDENCE

Our final appeal is not to the early church leaders, but to God, who by his Holy Spirit has put his seal upon the New Testament. By their spiritual content and by the claim of their human writers, the twenty-seven books of our New Testament form part of the 'God breathed' Scripture. See Book 2 chapter 2 in this series for the inspiration and inerrancy of Scripture. Anyone who has read the apocryphal and heretical writings produced in the first few centuries (see below in chapter 8) will immediately realise the enormous difference between these and the Gospels and the apostolic writing.

The sixteenth century Swiss Reformer and theologian John Calvin expressed well the significance of divine providence:

'Nothing, therefore, can be more absurd than the fiction, that the power of judging Scripture is in the Church, and that on her nod its certainty depends ... Scripture bears upon the face of it as clear evidence of its truth, as white and black do of their colour, sweet and bitter of their taste ... Our conviction of the truth of Scripture must be derived from a higher source than human conjectures, judgements or reasons: namely, the secret testimony of the Spirit.'[16]

The pattern for this relationship between the human and the divine is the way in which the Scriptures themselves were written. The true meaning of the Greek word *theopneustos* in 2 Timothy 3:16 reminds us that all Scripture is 'God-breathed'; yet it came through men moved by the Holy Spirit (2 Peter 1:21). It is this harmony of the active mind of the human writer and the sovereign direction of the Holy Spirit that provides our confidence in God's inerrant and infallible word. In the same way, we should never overlook the superintendence of God ensuring that only the books that he wanted would form part of the New Testament.

Carl Henry commented on this phenomenon of the divine intervention of God: 'The first observation to be made in an objective survey is the remarkably extensive agreement with which the early church distinguished

---

16 John Calvin, *Institutes of the Christian Religion*, Trans. Henry Beveridge (James Clark & Co. Ltd, London 1962. Orig. 1536), Book I, Ch. 7:2,4.

a particular and limited group of writings from all other literature ... and received them as uniquely inspired and of divine authority.'[17]

John Wenham expressed the same truth: 'Grounds of canonicity are to be found in an interplay of subjective and objective factors overruled by Divine Providence.'[18]

In the chapters that follow, it will be seen that long before we have a directory of twenty-seven books, we have twenty-seven books being used as Scripture. The books of the New Testament carried their own authority, and because of this they were recognised by the churches. The authority resided in the books themselves and not in the lists that they later entered.

---

17 Carl Henry, *God, Revelation and Authority*, Vol. IV, p. 440.

18 John W Wenham, *Christ and the Bible* (Tyndale Press, London 1972), p.126. More than a century earlier, the respected New Testament scholar, B F Westcott, referred to 'the guidance of Providence' in his detailed assessment of the development of the canon, *The Canon of the New Testament*, p. 293.

2. The Jews and their Bible—the books in the Old Testament

Jesus and the apostles were using for their Scripture the same books that the Jews had accepted centuries before.

Long before Jesus and the apostles, the Jews had a clearly defined body of Scripture that collectively could be summarized as the Torah or Law. They did not order them in the same way as our Old Testament, but the same books were there. Strictly, *The Law (Torah)* was the first five books, known as the Pentateuch which means 'five rolls'. *The Prophets (Nevi'im)* consisted of the Former Prophets (unusually for us these included Joshua, Judges, Samuel and Kings) and the Latter Prophets (Isaiah, Jeremiah, Ezekiel and the twelve smaller prophetic books). *The Writings (Ketuvim)* gathered up the rest. The total amounted to twenty-four books (sometimes counted as twenty-two) because many books, such as 1 and 2 Samuel, and Ezra-Nehemiah were counted as one.

It is not known exactly when the canon of the Old Testament was settled. However, if we accept the reasonable position that each of the books was written close to the time of its history—the first five at the time of Moses, the historical books close to the period they record, the psalms of David during his lifetime, and the prophets written at the time they were given—then the successive stages of acceptance into the canon of Scripture is not hard to fix. The Jews generally held to this position. Clearly, when the Law was rediscovered in the time of Josiah it was accepted as having the stamp of God's authority upon it (2 Kings 23:3). Contrary to the views of some, there is no reason to assume that this was the first time the Law had been recognised, still less was written, as Scripture. We also know that it was customary for the words of the prophets to be written down at the time they were given (eg Jeremiah 36:2,4). See Book 1 chapter 6 in this series for detailed evidence of the Old Testament books written at the time they record.

Most modern suggestions of a late date for the final acceptance of the Old Testament canon rely on the fragile theories that the Bible books were written very much later than the periods they reflect. The idea that there was a threefold time sequence in the acceptance of the canon on the basis of the words of Jesus: 'Everything must be fulfilled that is written about me in the Law of Moses, the Prophets and the Psalms' (Luke 24:44), is without any foundation beyond speculation. There are times when the entire Hebrew canon is summarized as 'Law'. Jesus did this when he referred the Jews to 'your Law' and then quoted from Psalm 82 (John 10:34).

The evidence of the Old Testament

What the Old Testament says about itself is significant in determining the way it was accepted as the word of God.

MOSES IS ALWAYS SEEN AS THE MOUTHPIECE AND SCRIBE OF GOD

Throughout the Old Testament there is agreement that the first five books of the Bible were written by Moses. Frequently we find Moses himself writing in a book the laws, activities, the history and even the geography of Israel's wilderness wandering (Exodus 24:4; 34:27–28, Numbers 33:2 and Deuteronomy 31:9,22,24). When Joshua received the leadership of Israel on the death of Moses, he was careful to read all the books of Moses to the people (Joshua 8:31–35); we may assume that Joshua added the final chapter to Deuteronomy which records the death of Moses. After Joshua, came the sad years of Israel's disobedience during the period of the Judges; however even here, a century after Moses' death, there is a reference to the commandments given through Moses (Judges 3:4).

The same 'Law of Moses' was handed down through the line of the kings of Judah. David gave it to his son Solomon (1 Kings 2:3). Amaziah reacted to the children of his father's murderers 'in accordance with what is written in the Book of the Law of Moses' (2 Kings 14:6). The accounts of the reigns of Hezekiah (2 Kings 18:6), Manasseh (2 Kings 21:8), Josiah

(2 Kings 23:25), Jehoshaphat (2 Chronicles 17:9), Jehoiada (2 Chronicles 23:18) and Amaziah (2 Chronicles 25:4) all contain references to the 'Law of the LORD' or 'the Law of Moses', which was understood to be the same.

After the kings, came the exile in Babylon, and the prophets of the exile continued to remind the people of the law of Moses (see Ezekiel 7:26; Daniel 9:11,13). When they returned from exile there are ten references in Ezra and Nehemiah to the use they made of the Law of Moses (eg. Ezra 6:18; Nehemiah 8:1).

References to God's Law in the book of Psalms are so numerous that the reader can find them at a casual glance. Psalm 119 is the greatest example of this, where only five of the 176 verses do not contain a direct reference to the Law. The prophets Isaiah (8:20) and Jeremiah (8:8) both refer to the Law. Among the other prophets, Hosea, Amos, Micah, Zephaniah, Haggai and Zechariah all refer to the Law, and Malachi, the last book of the Old Testament, urged the nation, on behalf of God: 'Remember the law of my servant Moses, the decrees and laws I gave him at Horeb [Sinai] for all Israel' (Malachi 4:4).

The Jews, throughout their history, accepted the books of Moses as the Law of God.

MOSES EXPECTED HIS BOOKS TO BE COPIED AND KEPT

Moses spoke of the time, many centuries ahead, when Israel would choose a king to rule over them. One of the first acts that the new king should carry out was described in this way:

'When he takes the throne of his kingdom, he is to write for himself on a scroll a copy of this law, taken from that of the priests, who are Levites. It is to be with him, and he is to read it all the days of his life so that he may learn to revere the LORD his God and follow carefully all the words of this law and these decrees...' (Deuteronomy 17:18–19).

Moses fully expected his words to form part of Israel's religious life for ever, and because of this he not only wrote a book of the law (Exodus 24:4), but read it to the people (Exodus 24:7) and placed a copy for safe-keeping beside the Ark of the Covenant (Deuteronomy 31:24–26).

However, Moses did not assume that God's revelation to men would come to an end when he himself died. God had already told him: 'I will raise up for them a prophet like you from among their brothers; I will put my words in his mouth, and he will tell them everything I command him' (Deuteronomy 18:18). Moses also warned the people against false prophets (vv. 20–22).

THE PROPHETS WITNESSED TO THE AUTHORITY OF EACH OTHER

There was a long tradition of writing among the prophets of Israel, including evidence of some of the prophets being commanded to write down their message (Jeremiah 30:2; Habakkuk 2:2). What is more important is the fact that many of the prophets referred to each other's ministry and reminded the people that it was a word from God. Here are some examples.

- Jeremiah 26:18 reminded the people of a verse found in Micah 3:12. Micah was a prophet who began his ministry one hundred and twenty years before Jeremiah.

- Jeremiah 28:8 spoke approvingly of the authority of 'the prophets who preceded you and me.'

- Ezekiel 38:17 referred to the prophecies of Isaiah concerning the enemies of Israel. Isaiah was prophesying some two hundred years before Ezekiel.

- Daniel 9:2 reveals that Daniel had been reading from Jeremiah 25:11–12.

- Zechariah 1:4–6 contains a reference to Isaiah 1:16; 31:6 and also to passages in Jeremiah and Ezekiel. What is particularly important about this passage in Zechariah is the comment by the prophet that although those who prophesied to 'your forefathers' have all died (v 5), yet the words of God through the prophets have outlived both prophets and fathers (v. 6). Here is a clear witness to the continuing value and authority of prophecy.

The evidence outside the Bible

THE TESTIMONY OF JOSEPHUS, PHILO AND THE TALMUD TO THE HEBREW CANON

Josephus (AD 37–100), the Jewish first century historian who joined the revolt against the Roman occupation and then switched sides, clearly stated in his defence of Judaism that, unlike the Greeks, the Jews did not have many books:

'From Artaxerxes to our own time the complete history has been written but has not been deemed worthy of equal credit with the earlier records because of the failure of the exact succession of the prophets. ... For we have not an innumerable multitude of books among us, disagreeing from and contradicting one another [as the Greeks have] but only twenty-two books, which contain the records of all the past times; which are justly believed to be divine, and of them five belong to Moses ... but as to the time from the death of Moses till the reign of Artaxerxes King of Persia ... the prophets, who were after Moses, wrote down what was done in their time in thirteen books. The remaining four books contain hymns to God and precepts for the conduct of human life.' [19]

His twenty-two books are the same as our thirty-nine in the Old Testament since, as mentioned above, many that we separate are counted as one book. In fact, the twelve prophets at the end of our Old Testament were placed together as one under the title 'The Book of the Twelve'.

Josephus added that during the many ages that had already passed, no Jew would be so bold 'as either to add anything to them, to take anything from them, or to make any change in them. But it is become natural to all Jews immediately, and from their very birth, to esteem these books to contain Divine doctrines.' [20]

For Josephus and the Jews of this time, the Hebrew Scriptures came from God through Moses and the prophets, and when the line of the prophets came to an end with Haggai, Zechariah and Malachi, God's revelation through Scripture ceased. Josephus listed the books, and

19 Josephus, *Against Apion*, 1.8.
20 Josephus, *Against Apion*, 1.42.

continued that the reason why the same authority is not given to the history written after the time of Artaxerxes (Xerxes, to whom Esther was queen) is because 'there has not been an exact succession of prophets since that time'.[21]

A little before Josephus, **Philo** (25 BC–AD 50) similarly commented that the Jews: 'Have not altered even a single word of what had been written by him [Moses], but would rather endure to die a thousand times, than yield to any persuasion contrary to his laws and customs.'[22] Philo's writings reveal some two thousand quotations from the Pentateuch, and although he does not provide us with a list of canonical books, most of the Old Testament books are included in his work. He certainly never quoted from the *Apocrypha*.

The Babylonian Talmud (*Baba Batra*) is a collection of commentaries and teaching by the rabbis (teachers) and generally dated between AD 70 and 200. It contains a statement that supports the view of Josephus: 'After the latter prophets, Haggai, Zechariah and Malachi, the Holy Spirit departed from Israel.' *Baba Batra* lists twenty-four books of the Hebrew Scriptures which are the same as our Old Testament. For the Jew, God's revelation through Scripture ended at Malachi. Various traditions taught that either Ezra or Nehemiah was responsible for collecting (not choosing) the accepted books of recognised Hebrew Scripture; when prophecy ceased, the canon was complete.

The well-established tradition that Ezra, around 400 BC, collected the accepted books and had them accurately copied, is confirmed by many scholars. John Wenham concludes, 'There is no reason to doubt that the Canon of the Old Testament is substantially Ezra's canon, just as the Pentateuch was substantially Moses' canon.'[23]

---

21 Bruce points out that Josephus did allow the existence of prophets but not in the line of the biblical seers and thus not with additional Scripture. F F Bruce, *The Canon of Scripture* (InterVarsity Press, Illinois 1988), p. 33.

22 Quoted by Eusebius, the first Christian historian writing in the mid-fourth century, *The Preparation for the Gospel*, Book 8, ch. 6. Translated by E H Gifford (Oxford 1903).

23 John Wenham, *Christ and the Bible*. (WIPF and Stock Publishers, Oregon. First published 1972), p. 134.

What happened at Jamnia?

Between AD 90 and 100, a group of Jewish scholars met at Jamnia in Israel to consider matters relating to the Hebrew Scriptures. There are no contemporary records of their deliberations and our knowledge is therefore left to the comments of later Rabbis. It was once assumed that 'Here the books of the Jewish Scriptures were decided.'[24] This is not only in conflict with the testimony of Josephus and Philo, but it is now generally accepted that Jamnia was not a council, nor did it pronounce on the Jewish canon; rather it was an assembly (some prefer the word academy) that examined and discussed the canon. The purpose of Jamnia was not to decide which books would be included among the sacred writings for the Jews, but to examine those that were already accepted.[25]

One of the greatest Jewish scholars, Rabbi Akiba ben Joseph (AD 50–135) commented on the deliberations at Jamnia: 'If there has been any dispute, it referred only to Ecclesiastes'. He himself considered that the Song of Solomon, which had been long accepted, was a 'holy of holies' among the Hebrew Scriptures.[26]

Since the Hebrew Scriptures circulated as individual scrolls, it is not possible to say precisely when they were viewed as a complete and final body of sacred writings. However, what is certain is that well before the Qumran community, who copied what are known as the *Dead Sea Scrolls* from the mid-second century BC, (see Book 4 chapter 2 in this series), pious Jews recognised that the Scriptures were complete and that the voice of the prophets had fallen silent.

---

24 Dennis C. Duling and Norman Perrin, *The New Testament, an Introduction: Proclamation and Parenesis, Myth and History* (Harcourt Brace Jovanovich 1982), p. 31. See also Charles Gore, Henry Leighton Goudge, Alfred Guillaume, *A New Commentary on Holy Scripture: Including the Apocrypha Book* (Macmillan 1936).

25 This is now widely accepted. See for example R. Beckwith, *The Old Testament Canon of the New Testament Church* (SPCK. London 1985), p. 276. Also A Bentzen, *Introduction to the Old Testament* (Copenhagen 1948), Vol. 1, p. 31. Bruce Metzger, *The Canon of the New Testament* (Oxford University Press. Oxford 1987), p. 110. John Wenham, *Christ and the Bible* (Tyndale Press, London 1972), pp. 138–139.

26 Quoted in William Robertson Smith *The Old Testament in the Jewish Church*. A series of lectures 1895. Lecture 6, p. 412.

Challenges to the canon among the Jews was unknown. Significantly, the Jewish scholars at Jamnia, like the later Christian leaders, had more material they could have chosen if they had wanted to. Apart from the *Apocrypha*, there were other writings around, such as the book of *Enoch*, the *Psalms of Solomon* and the *Martyrdom of Isaiah*—around seventeen books in all according to one scholar.[27]

The *Apocrypha*

Toby, Judith and Susanna are old English Christian names that reveal the influence the *Apocrypha* once had upon English social life. 'Tobit' and 'Judith' are books within the *Apocrypha*, and in the 'History of Susanna' it is Daniel the prophet who saves Susanna from an unjust death. The *Apocrypha* has had undoubted influence on the art and poetry of the west—familiar hymns such as 'Now thank we all, our God' and 'It came upon a midnight clear' were evidently influenced by passages in the *Apocrypha*.

Four hundred years of history, important in the life of the Jewish nation, covers the period from the close of Malachi to the Gospel of Matthew. During this 'inter-testamental period', fourteen of the books (fifteen if the 'Prayer of Jeremiah' is included separately from 'Baruch') were written. They are collectively known as the *Apocrypha*. The title *Apocrypha* is taken from a Greek adjective meaning 'hidden'.

The *Apocrypha* is a mixture of history and legend. It is a useful collection of books to help us understand the hopes of the Jews for the coming of the Messiah and their struggle to remain pure and loyal to their religion in an alien society. Some of the books that make up the *Apocrypha* are concerned with stories already found in the Bible. For example, '1 and 2 Esdras' deal with the events of rebuilding the city after the exile, recorded in Ezra and Nehemiah. 'The Rest of Esther' retells the Bible story of Esther, whilst 'Tobit' and 'Judith' are accounts of life after the destruction of Jerusalem by Nebuchadnezzar; and 'The Song of the

---

27 R H Charles, *The Apocrypha and Pseudepigrapha of the Old Testament* (Clarendon Press. Oxford 1913), 2 vols. Though some would add more than seventeen.

Three Holy Children' is concerned with the three friends thrown into the furnace by Nebuchadnezzar. 'The History of Susanna' and 'Bel and the Dragon' are both stories of Daniel. The two books of 'Maccabees' record some of the Maccabean wars, before the birth of Christ, when many nationalistic Jews fought hard for their independence against the Syrians and later the Romans.

SHOULD WE INCLUDE THE *APOCRYPHA*?

The *Apocrypha* has never been accepted by Protestant Christians as part of the Bible. In 1643 a preacher before the Commonwealth Parliament in London denounced 'that wretched *Apocrypha*'. However, others have been more generous towards it, whilst never accepting its authority. Even John Bunyan, the courageous Puritan Baptist author, spoke of the benefit he had gained by reading from Ecclesiasticus.

On the other hand, the Roman Catholic church attributes to some of the *Apocrypha* the same authority as it does to the Bible. They include: 'Tobit', 'Judith', 'Wisdom', 'Sirach', 'Baruch', 'I and II Maccabees' and the additional stories of Daniel and Esther. The two books of 'Esdras' and the 'Prayer of Manasses' are not considered canonical. For a long time, the Roman church was divided on the issue. In AD 405 Pope Innocent I endorsed the *Apocrypha*, even though at the same time Jerome, who was responsible for translating the Bible into Latin, wanted to exclude it. In AD 600 another pope excluded it, as did Cardinal Ximenes in the sixteenth century. Finally, at the Council of Trent in 1546, Rome made up its mind and a curse was placed upon all who reject the *Apocrypha*.

The Russian and Greek Orthodox churches are less decided in their attitude towards the *Apocrypha*. Whilst sometimes making a distinction between the *Apocrypha* and Scripture, in practice they treat them as equal, and most Orthodox priests will insist that the *Apocrypha* is part of their Bible, even though there are few official statements to this effect. Some Orthodox Bibles include the books of the *Apocrypha* scattered through the Old Testament, which implies an equal status.

Because it was translated into Greek in the third century BC along with the Old Testament Scriptures, some of the early church leaders referred to the *Apocrypha* in much the same way that they quoted from the Old Testament itself. On the other hand, many of the leaders, like Melito of Sardis, Origen and Athanasius of Alexandria, Cyril of Jerusalem and John of Damascus all rejected the *Apocrypha* as being inferior to the Scriptures. However, there were sufficient leaders in its favour, including the influential Augustine of Hippo, for many in the church, both in the east and in the west, to accept the *Apocrypha* as Scripture right up until the time of the Reformation in the sixteenth century. But there was little certainty about it, and much confusion.

REASONS FOR REJECTING THE *APOCRYPHA*

1. Jesus and the New Testament writers were constantly quoting from the Old Testament as authoritative, but not once did they refer to the *Apocrypha* in this way, although they certainly had access to it. It was not that they avoided reference to other writings, because Jude 14–15 refers to the book of Enoch, written during the time of the *Apocrypha*, and Paul quotes from Greek poets (Acts 17:28; 1 Corinthians 15:33; Titus 1:12).

   There are a few expressions in the New Testament that are found in the *Apocrypha*, for example: 'I gathered you together as a hen gathers her chickens under her wings' (2 Esdras 1:30, compare Matthew 23:37). 'The innumerable multitude of angels' (2 Esdras 6:3, compare Hebrews 12:22). 'There was a voice that spoke, and the sound of it was like the sound of many waters' (2 Esdras 6:17, compare Revelation 1:15). Hebrews 1:3 may reflect 'The Wisdom of Solomon' 7:26 where wisdom is described as 'The brightness of the everlasting light, the unspotted mirror of the power of God, and the image of his goodness'. Some of these expressions may have been in common use, and it is likely that Jesus and the apostles, familiar with the language of the *Apocrypha* employed it to their own end. However, the books of the *Apocrypha* were never mentioned as the source or used as an authority. An allusion does not imply authority.

2. The first century Jewish historian, Josephus, and the Jewish Talmud were quite clear that the books of the *Apocrypha* formed no part of the Old Testament. Josephus believed that nothing could be added to or taken from the canon of the Hebrew Scriptures.[28]

3. The community who copied out the Dead Sea Scrolls never referred to these books with the special phrases, 'It is written', or 'God says', and therefore clearly they did not accept them as part of the Hebrew Scriptures.

4. Philo, the Jewish Philosopher writing from Alexandria in AD 40, quoted from, or referred to, all but five Old Testament books, but the *Apocrypha* was never mentioned or quoted. Similarly, the Jewish Council of Jamnia, five decades after Philo, rejected the *Apocrypha*.

5. None of the books of the *Apocrypha* ever claims inspiration or a divine origin. The phrase 'Hear the word of the Lord', so familiar in the Old Testament, does not occur in the *Apocrypha*. The writers were careful to avoid their work being confused with Scripture. On three occasions, the first book of Maccabees states that a prophet was no longer available in Israel. In 1 Maccabees 9:27 the writer records the terrible sufferings of the Maccabean wars and claims, 'So there was a great affliction in Israel, unlike anything since the time a prophet had ceased to be seen among them' (see also 1 Maccabees 4:46; 14:41).

6. Some parts of the *Apocrypha* contain historical errors and even contradict the teaching of the Old Testament. The 'Prayer of Manasseh' includes the statement: 'You therefore, Oh Lord, who is the God of the just, have not appointed repentance to the just, to Abraham and Isaac and Jacob, which have not sinned against you...' All scholars admit the many errors in 'Tobit' and 'Judith'. The opening verse of 'Judith' refers to the Babylonian king Nebuchadnezzar as king in 'Nineveh' (the capital of the Assyrian empire and totally destroyed by the Babylonians

---

28 Josephus, *Against Apion*. Translated by William Whiston (Ward, Lock & Co. London. No date given),1.8 where Josephus claims the Jews have only 22 books (equivalent to our 36). See also 1.42.

in 612 BC). 2 Maccabees 12:40–45 claims not only the right, but the great value, of praying for the dead, 'that they might be delivered from sin'—a theology found nowhere in Scripture but valuable to the Roman Catholic church. Although the two books of the 'Maccabees' are of historical value, most of the stories in the *Apocrypha* are fables with little historical base.

7. In AD 170 Melito, the leader of the church at Sardis, travelled to Jerusalem to assure himself of the exact limit of the Jewish Scriptures. He came back with a list precisely as our Old Testament, with the exception of Esther, which he seemed to have omitted in error and, for some reason, added 'The Wisdom of Solomon'. Augustine is an important exception by including the *Apocrypha*, but even he admitted that the Jews did not accept the *Apocrypha* as part of the canon of the Old Testament.

All the available evidence is that the Jews, Jesus and the apostles, the Reformers and the Puritans never accepted the *Apocrypha* as part of Scripture. The earliest English translations of John Wycliffe (1380) did include the *Apocrypha* as a separate section, though with an introductory note that they are 'without the authority of the Bible', and the same was true of the Dutch translations (1526) and German-Swiss (1527–1529). Tyndale did not live to complete the translation of the Old Testament, and therefore John Rogers, who compiled *Matthew's Bible* (1537) from Tyndale's work, simply added the translations of Miles Coverdale to complete the Old Testament and the *Apocrypha*.

The *Geneva Bible* (1560)—so loved by the early Protestants and the Puritans—included the *Apocrypha*, though with a disclaimer, until an edition appeared in 1599 without it. The *King James Version* (1611) originally contained the *Apocrypha*, although the Church of England in the *Thirty-Nine Articles* of 1563 had rejected them from belonging to the canon. The Puritans in their *Westminster Confession of Faith* in 1647, concluded, 'The books commonly called *Apocrypha*, not being of divine inspiration, are no part of the canon of the Scripture; and therefore are of no authority in the Church of God, nor to be any otherwise approved, or made use of, than other human writings.'[29]

THE EVIDENCE OF THE *SEPTUAGINT* FOR THE *APOCRYPHA*

The Greek translation of the Hebrew Old Testament, the *Septuagint*, commenced around the middle of the third century BC. The word *Septuagint* means 'seventy' and refers to the tradition that seventy scholars were involved in its translation. As Greek was the common language across the Roman empire, the *Septuagint* became the Old Testament text used by many Jews in exile and in Jerusalem (Josephus included), and was significantly used by the apostles and the early church (for more on the *Septuagint* see also in this series Book 2 chapter 4 and Book 4 chapter 2).

The only complete copies of the *Septuagint* available today are from the Christian era in the fourth and fifth centuries AD and these do contain many of the books of the *Apocrypha*. However, it is highly unlikely that the original texts of the *Septuagint* could have included all the apocryphal books, since it is doubtful whether they had all been written so early as 250 BC. Certainly Josephus was apparently unaware of their inclusion when he limited the Jewish Scriptures to the equivalent of our thirty-nine books. If the *Apocrypha* was present in the copies of the *Septuagint* used by Jesus and the apostles, it is even more significant that they never once quoted or directly referred to it.[30]

The *Dead Sea Scrolls*

The collection of scrolls, in various stages of decay, that became available since the discovery of the first texts in 1947 near Wadi Qumran close by the Dead Sea, may not help us greatly in our search for the canon of the Old Testament. No definitive list appears from the community, and even if it did, it would not necessarily tell us what mainstream orthodox Judaism

---

29 For a full discussion on the *Apocrypha* in early editions of English Bibles see David Daniell, *The Bible in English* (Yale University Press, New Haven and London 2003).
30 For a more detailed discussion of the *Septuagint* see F F Bruce, *The Canon of Scripture*. (InterVarsity Press, Illinois 1988), pp. 43–54.

believed. See Book 4 chapter 2 in this series for more on the importance of the Dead Sea Scrolls.

However, all Old Testament books are represented among the Qumran collection with the exception of Esther, and it is generally agreed that the Law and the Prophets were regarded as authoritative Scripture. In fact, it is only the position of Ruth, Song of Songs, Ecclesiastes, Ezra-Nehemiah, Chronicles and Esther for which the evidence is insufficient one way or the other.

On the other hand, very little of the *Apocrypha* has been discovered among the scrolls, and it is never expounded in Qumran texts. The Qumran community only wrote their commentaries about biblical books. Despite suggestions by critical scholars to the contrary, there is no evidence, not even from the *Dead Sea Scrolls*, that there were any other books contending for a place within the Old Testament canon, or that any of our present books should not be there.

The *Dead Sea Scrolls* reflect something that is found in all Jewish writing at this time and that is that whilst no list of canonical books is offered, whenever the canonical books are quoted or referred to, their divine and ultimate authority is assumed. Other books may carry authority, such as the 'Community Rule' (known also as the 'Manual of Discipline') of the Dead Sea community, but this did not give it the status of God's word. This is precisely what we find in the writing of the early Christian leaders: they do not provide us with a neat list of books that form the New Testament canon, but they quote and refer to them frequently and treat them—and only these—as ultimate authority.

The *Samaritan Pentateuch*

The Samaritans, despised by the Jews for historic reasons, adopted a very limited canon, and used only their edited version of the Pentateuch (the first five books of the Hebrew Bible). This cannot be offered as evidence of a 'fluid' canon since the Samaritans formed no part of orthodox Judaism for whom, as we have seen, the canon was never in serious doubt.

The evidence of the New Testament

If the test for an Old Testament Bible book was that it came from Moses or the prophets, that leaves large parts of the Old Testament that would appear to fall outside this definition. However, this was apparently no problem to Jesus or the Jews of his day. Jesus summarized the whole of the Old Testament as 'Moses and the Prophets' (Luke 16:29,31).

In Matthew 13:35 Jesus quoted from Psalm 78:2 and claimed that it came from 'the prophet'; no Jew would have suggested that this was a mistake. In Luke 11:50–51, Jesus included among the list of prophets: Abel (Genesis 4) and Zechariah (2 Chronicles 24:20–21, though this was not the prophet of the Bible book of this name). A prophet did not simply foretell the future, but more especially gave out God's word, and therefore spoke as the voice of God. Under this definition not only Moses, but David and Solomon, Ezra and Nehemiah and others were also prophets. Even those books whose authors we cannot be sure of—like Judges, Ruth, Job and Chronicles—were apparently accepted by Jesus and the Jews as coming from the hand of the prophets.

Jesus set the pattern for his disciples when he claimed 'it stands written' (Matthew 4:4,6,10) and 'Scripture cannot be broken' (John 10:35). The New Testament writers accepted the authority of the Old Testament without question and without addition and, like Israel before them, they considered it to be God speaking 'to our forefathers through the prophets' (Hebrews 1:1). The fact that the New Testament writers quote from the Hebrew Scriptures some two hundred and fifty times and make over nine hundred allusions from all but six books, shows that the New Testament writers had no difficulty in accepting the Old Testament canon. Significantly, whenever the apostles quoted from the Old Testament they used such introductions as 'Scripture says', 'God says', 'it is written' and Paul's 'according to the Scriptures'. Paul had no doubt that the Jews were 'entrusted with the very words [the oracles] of God' (Romans 3:2). These phrases are never used of any other literature.

The only time that an apostle quoted from a Jewish book other than the Old Testament was Jude's quotation from the *Book of Enoch* (only one third of which has survived and which is not part of the *Apocrypha*).

Jude simply quoted from a piece of literature, and he does not tell us his source and certainly lays no claim to its authority (Jude 14,15).[31] Paul similarly made a brief reference to the pagan writers Cleanthes (Acts 17:28), Menander (1 Corinthians 15:33) and Epimenides (Titus 1:12), without implying any divine authority.

In the light of all this, it is indefensible to suggest that the canon of the Old Testament was not fixed in the time of the apostles or the early church.[32] Carl Henry wisely concludes: 'The church inherited the Old Testament, and Jesus defended, encouraged and exemplified faithful submission to these writings as an inspired canon.'[33]

The early Christian leaders and their Old Testament

The churches in the first three centuries were mainly using the *Septuagint* for their Old Testament and, as we have seen, the earliest copies of the *Septuagint* available today go back only to the fifth century AD and they include the apocryphal books. There was certainly, therefore, some possibility for confusion.

Melito, the bishop of Sardis, died in AD 180 and was the first to provide us with a list of Old Testament books that many of the churches in the East were using—it is identical to our canon. Origen was born around the time of Melito's death, and he included the apocryphal *Letter of Jeremiah* as part of the prophet Jeremiah, although many scholars consider this was an oversight by Origen. Athanasius of Alexandria followed Origen although, since he was clear that the *Apocrypha* formed no part of the divinely inspired canon, it would appear that Athanasius was thoughtlessly copying Origen.

---

31 Although translations of Enoch were known in Ethiopic and Greek, Aramaic fragments were discovered among the *Dead Sea Scrolls* (Q4). The *Book of Enoch* is generally thought to be dated around 200 BC. It claims to be prophecies of Enoch (Genesis 5). Jude clearly quotes from Enoch 1:9. Some maintain that there are allusions to the book even in the teaching of Jesus, but this is doubtful.

32 A helpful response to those who claim otherwise will be found in *Hermeneutics, Authority and Canon*, ed. Carson and Woodbridge (InterVarsity Press, London 1986), pp. 308–310.

33 Carl F H Henry, *God, Revelation and Authority* (Paternoster, Carlisle 1999. orig. USA 1979), Vol. IV. p. 407.

Among the churches of the West, the picture is muddied by the fact that Tertullian, bishop of Carthage, considered that some of the books of the *Apocrypha*, and even *Enoch* and the *Sibylline Oracles*,[34] might be inspired. The early church leaders were often far less precise in their terminology and therefore at times they may seem to attribute a divine origin to books that they did not consider to be part of the canon. They were unaware of the difficulty this would cause to later historians and theologians. Whilst it is true that some of the leaders quoted from the *Apocrypha*, though very rarely compared to their use of the Old Testament books, there is no evidence that they recognised these books as equal to the Old Testament.[35]

It was left to Jerome in the mid-fourth century who, when he began to translate the Old Testament into Latin, recognised the wisdom of using the Hebrew Scriptures rather than the Greek *Septuagint* and consequently objected to translating the *Apocrypha*. However, Augustine did include some of the apocryphal books, and the issue rumbled on throughout the middle ages until, as we have seen, eventually the Roman Catholic Council of Trent in 1546 endorsed much of the *Apocrypha*.

See Book 4 chapter 1 in this series for the *Apocrypha* in the story of our English Bible.

---

34 A collection of Jewish and Christian poems composed between 200 BC and AD 250. See J J Collins, *The Old Testament Pseudepigrapha*, ed. Charlesworth, pp. 317–472.
35 This is a point made firmly by John W Wenham in *Christ and the Bible*, pp. 146–147

3. The early Christians and their Bible

During the first four centuries, no church council decided what books would form the New Testament canon, they simply acknowledged what the churches were already widely using.

According to Luke, even before the ink was dry on the scrolls of the apostolic Gospels, others were drawing up their own account of 'the things that have been fulfilled among us' (Luke 1:1); but it was eyewitness accounts that mattered to Luke. His careful investigation (v. 3) was typical of the early church leaders who followed. They did not thoughtlessly accept all that claimed to be apostolic. The evidence will show how careful the early church leaders were. This chapter is largely a summary of the one that follows. Conclusions are drawn here, the evidence for which will be seen in the next chapter.

The Christian church was never without a Bible. The entire Hebrew Scriptures were accepted as the divinely inspired and authoritative word of God. Therefore, 'The Christian church did not require to form for itself the idea of a "canon" … it inherited this idea from the Jewish church.'[36]

The beginning of a New Testament canon

Long before the churches were eager to obtain copies of the letters from the apostles, those writers themselves were convinced that what they wrote was equal in authority to the prophets of the Old Testament. The prophets declared what was 'revealed to them', and so the gospel was preached through the apostles 'by the Holy Spirit sent from heaven' (1 Peter 1:12).

---

36 This point was made long ago by B B Warfield in *The Formation of the Canon of the New Testament*, published by the American Sunday School Union 1892. Published in *The Inspiration and Authority of the Bible* (Presbyterian and Reformed Publishing Company, Philadelphia 1948), p. 411.

Paul was convinced that what he spoke was 'not in words taught us by human wisdom but in words taught by the Spirit' (1 Corinthians 2:13); which meant that his instructions were 'by the authority of the Lord Jesus' (1 Thessalonians. 4:2). The apostles knew themselves to be part of the continuing revelation of Scriptures given by men who 'spoke from God as they were carried along by the Holy Spirit' (2 Peter 1:21).

It is equally clear that the apostles expected their letters to be read and passed around the churches, even when the original was addressed to a particular congregation (Colossians 4:16). See Book 2 chapter 5 in this series for more on the authority claimed by the apostles. It is therefore not surprising to find one of the earliest Christian leaders following this precise pattern. Polycarp, who had been a disciple of the apostle John and was martyred in AD 155, wrote a brief letter to the church at Philippi and quoted from Ephesians 4:26 in the following way:

'For I trust that you are well versed in the Sacred Scriptures, and that nothing is hid from you … It is declared then in these Scriptures, "Be ye angry, and sin not," and, "Let not the sun go down upon your wrath."' [37]

Polycarp had no doubt that Paul's letter to the Ephesians was 'Sacred Scripture', and he assumed that the Christians at Philippi believed the same. Elsewhere he referred to the 'oracles' of the Lord, using precisely the word that Paul had used to refer to the Hebrew Scriptures in Romans 3:2. Clearly referring to the first epistle of John, Polycarp linked the 'testimony of the cross' with the 'oracles of the Lord':

'For whosoever does not confess that Jesus Christ has come in the flesh, is antichrist; and whosoever does not confess the testimony of the cross, is of the devil; and whosoever perverts the oracles of the Lord to his own lusts, and says that there is neither a resurrection nor a judgment, he is the first-born of Satan.' [38]

Possibly around the same time, an epistle known as the *Second Epistle of Clement to the Corinthians* (which is generally considered not to be

---

37 Polycarp, *To the Philippians*, Ch.12.
38 As above, Ch. 7.

from the hand of Clement) quoted from Isaiah and followed it by: 'Again another scripture says, "I came not to call the righteous, but sinners"', which is taken from Mark 2:17 or Luke 5:32.[39]

As we will see in the next chapter, whilst there is evidence of all the New Testament books being used early in the second century, there is no evidence yet of a definitive list of books before the middle of that century. However, the early Christian leaders clearly accepted the New Testament Gospels and letters as divinely inspired and therefore authoritative. The way they quoted from and referred to the four Gospels and the letters of the apostles, reveals a uniqueness that is afforded to no other writings; and they often contrasted the authority of the Bible books with their own.

Polycarp referred to the apostolic books as the 'oracles' of the Lord. Ignatius, who was martyred around AD 115, is typical of the way the church Fathers linked the 'Gospels and the Apostles' with the 'Law and the Prophets'. Writing to the Philadelphian church Ignatius commented:

'While I flee to the Gospel as to the flesh of Jesus Christ, and to the apostles as the presbytery of the Church. I do also love the prophets as those who announced Christ, and as being partakers of the same Spirit with the apostles. ... The prophets and the apostles receive from God, through Jesus Christ, one and the same Holy Spirit, who is good, and sovereign, and true, and the Author of [saving] knowledge. For there is one God of the Old and New Testament.'[40]

That reference to the 'New Testament' in the context of the Old, is an indication of a growing collection of literature corresponding to the Hebrew Scriptures.

Similarly, to the Christians at Smyrna Ignatius wrote, 'but we should give heed to the Prophets, and especially to the Gospel, wherein the passion is shown unto us and the resurrection is accomplished.'[41] Whilst he does not name the 'Gospels' and the 'Apostles', Ignatius clearly possessed copies that would be recognised as such when he wrote to the Magnesians: 'Do

---

39 *Clement's Second letter to the Corinthians*, Ch. 2:8.
40 Ignatius, *Epistle to the Philadelphians*, Ch. 5.
41 Ignatius, *Epistle to the Smyrnaean*, Ch. 7:4.

your diligence therefore that you be confirmed in the ordinances of the Lord and of the Apostles.'[42]

When, a century later, Tertullian wrote of the Old and New Testaments, the Latin word he used was *instrumentum*, an instrument or tool. He referred also to 'The Law and the Prophets, with the Gospels and the Apostles.'[43] Clement of Alexandria, a contemporary of Tertullian, made the same distinction.

All this is strong evidence that a developing canon of the New Testament was accepted long before a list of recognised books was drawn up either by the author of the *Muratorian Canon* around AD 150 (see chapter 4) or by Eusebius almost two centuries later.

In other words, the canon precedes the lists. By this is meant that before we have a directory of twenty-seven books, we have twenty-seven books being quoted and referred to as Scripture—that is an important distinction. The canon, as a formal list of books, appears to have grown slowly over the first one hundred years of the Christian church, although the authority of most of the books that eventually composed the canon was accepted immediately by all except 'a respectable minority of the church'.[44]

The word 'canon' was not used to refer specifically to the books of the New Testament until sometime early in the fourth century when Athanasius referred to the *Shepherd of Hermas* as 'not belonging to the canon'. However, this implies that there was a clear idea of a canon before then. The thought was deep-rooted in the church through its use of the *Septuagint*, and the apostolic writings were regularly read in the worship of the churches. In the middle of the second century, Justin, in his *Apology* to the Emperor Titus, outlined a typical Christian service at which:

'On the day called Sunday, all who live in cities or in the country gather together to one place, and the memoirs of the apostles or the writings of the prophets are read,

---

42 Ignatius, *Epistle to the Magnesians*, Ch.12:8.
43 Tertullian, *De Praescriptione Haereticorum* (*On the Prescription of Heretics*), Ch.36.
44 So Warfield as above p.415.

as long as time permits; then, when the reader has ceased, the president verbally instructs, and exhorts to the imitation of these good things.'[45]

Although Justin does not mention it, other books were occasionally read at such meetings; these included the letters of Clement and the *Shepherd of Hermas*, but there is no evidence that they were placed on a par with the Gospels and the letters of the apostles, and they do not appear in the earliest lists of recognised books either. Carl Henry helpfully summarises the position: 'The first churches were therefore gifted not with a completed canon, but with a cumulative and culminating canon.'[46]

All this presupposes a recognition of what the 'memoirs of the apostles' actually were. That these books were early collected together is beyond serious dispute. The Chester Beatty Papyrus (P 46) is the oldest collection of Paul's letters to date—ten of them—and it is dated around AD 200, though some have moved this date before the close of the first century. See Book 4 chapter 3 in this series for the oldest manuscripts of the New Testament available today.

Oral or written records?

From all this, it defies logic to believe that an infant Christian church, reared on the conviction that the Old Testament Scriptures are the very words of God, should be satisfied for decades with mere oral traditions for their own authority. If the churches were eager to obtain copies of the letters of some of their early leaders, as we know they were, how much more enthusiastic would they be to obtain copies of apostolic writing; especially with the precedent of Colossians 4:16 to spur them: 'After this letter has been read to you, see that it is also read in the church of the Laodiceans and that you in turn read the letter from Laodicea.'

Furthermore, the consistent quotations by the church leaders from New Testament books is clear evidence that they possessed written collections. The fact that they did not always give their source is no more surprising than when a preacher today quotes from the Bible without providing book

---

45 *The first Apology of Justin Martyr to the Emperor Titus*, Ch. 47.
46 Carl Henry, *God, Revelation and Authority*. Vol. IV, p. 438.

or author. They were unaware that two millennia later scholars would be demanding a more exact code of reference.

Writing early in the fourth century, the church historian Eusebius, described the way the apostles left the church a written record of their gospel, and there is no reason to doubt the general truth of this claim:

'For Matthew, who had at first preached to the Hebrews, when he was about to go to other peoples, committed his Gospel to writing in his native tongue, and thus compensated those whom he was obliged to leave for the loss of his presence. And when Mark and Luke had already published their Gospels, they say that John, who had employed all his time in proclaiming the Gospel orally, finally proceeded to write for the following reason: The three Gospels already mentioned having come into the hands of all and into his own too, they say that he accepted them and bore witness to their truthfulness; but that there was lacking in them an account of the deeds done by Christ at the beginning of his ministry.'[47]

We should not forget that even oral tradition in the first century was very different from today. Not only did Jesus promise the Holy Spirit to aid the apostles' memory (John 14:26; 16:13), in fact memories in the ancient world were far more accurate and receptive than today. Xenophon (the Greek historian and philosopher in the fourth century BC) tells of one Niceratus who, as a boy, learnt the *Iliad* and *Odyssey* of Homer by heart— all twenty-four thousand lines.[48] That was not considered exceptional. Besides, during his three years of ministry Jesus repeated his teaching many times so that when his disciples went out preaching, they would accurately relay all that their Master had taught them. See Book 1 chapters 3 and 5 in this series for more on the importance of memory and writing in the first century.

The canon was complete when the last apostolic book was written, even though at the time the churches possessed no final list of these books. If we are to use the *Muratorian Canon* as our evidence, a canon of Scripture was evidently recognised by the mid second century; and it stayed that

---

47 Eusebius, *Church History*, Book III, Ch. 24:6.
48 Xenophon, *Symposium*, 3.6.

way. Even the doubts of Luther concerning the epistle of James and those of Zwingli concerning the Revelation of John, found no acceptance with the churches of the Reformation in the sixteenth century.

More clarity than confusion

The earliest collections of books did not make them authoritative, they were collected because they were already authoritative among most of the churches. Significantly, in all the lists of accepted books, those Gnostic books discovered in the so-called *Nag Hammadi Library* in 1945 (see chapter 8) were never considered as candidates—they were always known to be mischievous forgeries.

There is no evidence that the New Testament books came slowly to be recognised as authoritative and meanwhile jostled with an assortment of other literature before finally, after much wrangling and disagreement over a few centuries—and as much by luck as judgement—they were accepted as canonical by church decree sometime in the fourth century. All the available evidence runs contrary to this.

Contrary also to some current suggestions,[49] the 'canonical' books were accepted immediately by the churches that received them, and whilst a few of the books were recognised more slowly in parts of the empire, the evidence from the letters of the early church leaders—and they have left many hundreds of pages between them—is that they knew which books were 'apostolic' and which were not.[50] There is more confusion among modern critics than there ever was among the early church leaders. If they did not always use the words and phrases to describe them that we would like, such as: 'inspired', 'inerrant', 'infallible', 'canon', 'final authority'

---

49 This negative claim is made, for example, in an article in the *Biblical Archaeological Review* Sept/Oct 2016, pp. 41–47.

50 B B Warfield expressed this well in *The Formation of the Canon of the New Testament* as above p. 415: 'From the time of Irenaeus down, the church at large had the whole Canon as we now possess it. And though a section of the church may not have been satisfied of the apostolicity of a certain book or of certain books; and though afterwards doubts may have arisen in sections of the church as to the apostolicity of certain books (as eg of Revelation): yet in no case was it more than a respectable minority of the church which was slow in receiving, or which came afterwards to doubt, the credentials of any of the books that then as now constituted the Canon of the New Testament accepted by the church at large.'

and so on, it is because these did not form part of their vocabulary in this context. They did not use these words to describe the Old Testament Scriptures either.

What is significant is that from the earliest times we find the church leaders constantly using what we know as 'canonical' books either by direct quotation, paraphrase or inference, to support their arguments or encouragements—and they rarely use other books in the same way. From the beginning, for example, it is clear that there were no other Gospels than the four used by the churches right across the empire. The exceptions were the Gnostic and other cults who invented their own stories (see chapter 8). It is a matter of fact that none of these 'gospels' was ever a contender for a place in the canon.

Some books were recognised more slowly in parts of the empire: the letter to the Hebrews, the second epistle of Peter and the Apocalypse of John. Hebrews was at first accepted, and later questions were raised among the western churches because the Montanists (an early group of extreme Pentecostals) used it widely in their teaching. 2 Peter was written in a form that many considered unlike Peter's style. And the Apocalypse took longer to be accepted in the east because some were using it to support extravagant views of the millennium.

The modern idea that we cannot be sure of a completed canon and as a consequence we cannot have an authentic statement of Christian doctrine, would find no support from the leaders of the church in the first centuries.

Which came first: the church or the Bible?

It is largely, though not exclusively, a Roman Catholic argument that since the church came into existence before the Bible, it must be the Bible that is dependent upon the church for its authority. However, the same Lord who claimed that he would establish his church (Matthew 16:18) also promised that he would bring all things to the memory of the disciples for transmitting the truth (John 14:26; 16:13). His clear intention was for an authoritative and accurate Scripture for the church.

At no point in the history of the church in the first four centuries did a council decide what books the church should and should not have;

on the contrary, they simply acknowledged what the churches were already using. This is a significant difference. We shall see later what New Testament books were accepted by the churches long before councils met to discuss the issue. There was a remarkable degree of agreement among the churches regarding the authoritative books, as the Muratorian Canon from the mid-second century makes clear.

The Christian churches unanimously, and without debate, adopted the whole of the Hebrew Scriptures as the first and indispensable part of their canon. It was precisely in this way that the Jewish canon itself had come into being—by use and not by decree. It was only the Gnostic heretics, like Marcion, who dispensed with the Old Testament altogether. Even the liberal critic E J Goodspeed concluded, 'The church councils did not so much form the New Testament canon as recognize views about it that had taken shape in church usage.'[51]

How much more did the apostles write?

Not all that the apostles wrote has been preserved. Paul wrote letters to the Laodiceans, the Corinthians and others that have not come down to us (Colossians 4:16, 1 Corinthians 5:9 and 1 Thessalonians 5:27), and the only two or three personal letters (Philemon, and 2 and possibly 3 John) are not likely to be the total of all private correspondence by the apostles. This also has its parallel in the Hebrew Scriptures. The 'Book of the Wars of the Lord' (Numbers 21:14) has not come down to us and was never part of the canon of the Jews, nor was the 'Book of Jashar' (Joshua 10:13) or the 'Book of the Acts of Solomon' (1 Kings 11:41). There are many other missing books referred to in the Old Testament. For more on these 'lost' books see Book 1 chapter 6 in this series.

The first church historian, Eusebius, writing early in the fourth century, assured his readers that Paul wrote very few letters and that of the seventy disciples sent out by Jesus, only Matthew and John have left us a record. Eusebius maintained that John wrote his Gospel only after he had seen the

---

51 E J Goodspeed, *The Interpreter's Bible*, ed. GA Buttrick. (Abingdon Press, New York 1962), Vol. 1, p. 68.

other three.[52] Whilst Eusebius is not necessarily reliable in all this, there is no firm evidence to doubt him.

When Carl Henry claimed in 1979: 'There is little probability that early manuscripts that the Christian community felt unobliged to copy and to circulate widely will now be recovered',[53] he would not have to retract that even in the light of the *Nag Hammadi Library* and the *Judas Gospel*. These false writings were never even considered for circulation by the orthodox Christian community; they were the preserve of recognised heretical sects. Henry is right to conclude that even if a text that came from the hand of Paul was discovered today, we would not add it as a supplement to the Bible, since the canon of Scripture is closed—and has been for almost two thousand years.[54] In reality this issue will not trouble us, because if a letter claiming to come from the hand of Paul was discovered tomorrow, it would take until the end of time for the scholars to agree whether or not it was genuine!

---

52 As above, Eusebius, *Church History*, Book III, Ch. 24:6.
53 Carl Henry, *God, Revelation and Authority* (Paternoster Publishing. Carlisle 1999), Vol. IV, p. 409.
54 A point made also by F F Bruce, *The Canon of Scripture* (InterVarsity Press. Illinois 1988), pp. 278–279.

4. A growing collection

The early and steady acceptance of the books of the New Testament provides good evidence of the relative clarity of the formation of our New Testament canon.

In 1740 an Italian scholar, Ludovico Antonio Muratori, published a document he had discovered in a library in Milan. It was an eighth century copy of an original written in Latin some time before the middle of the second century AD, and it contains our oldest known list of New Testament books reflecting the position held by the church in Rome at that time.[55] Not all our canonical books are found in this list but none appears that ought not to be there—with one odd exception, the 'Wisdom of Solomon' which belongs in the *Apocrypha* and was never considered a New Testament book! The beginning and end of the copy are missing, and it commences with Luke as 'the third book of the Gospel'; clearly Matthew and Mark came first. The writer believed that 'all things are related by one imperial Spirit' in the Gospels.[56]

This *Muratorian Canon* not only lists the books of the New Testament, but adds comments on them indicating their origin and acceptance. For example, Luke is endorsed as having been on the staff of Paul. It includes the four Gospels, Acts, thirteen letters of Paul, Jude, two (perhaps all three) letters of John and the Revelation of John. These are accepted by 'the universal church'. This leaves out: 1 and 2 Peter, James and Hebrews. However, 1 Peter was widely accepted by this time and may be an oversight by the compiler (or the later copyist). A possible reference is made to the

---

55 G M Hahneman, *The Muratorian Fragment and the Development of the Canon* (Oxford University Press. Oxford 1992), suggested that it is a fourth century document; however, this is not generally accepted.

56 *The Muratorian Canon*, Trans. Roberts-Donaldson Translation: Ante-Nicene Fathers, vol. 5, Section 1. See also a translation in F F Bruce, *The Canon of Scripture* (InterVarsity Press, Illinois 1988), pp. 159–161 and Metzger, *The Canon of the New Testament* (OUP Clarendon Press, Oxford 1987), pp. 305–307.

Apocalypse of Peter with a note that it is not widely accepted; although this could be a reference to the letters of Peter.[57]

It contains also a list of heretical writers whose works are not to be used—these include Valentinus, Marcion and Basilides (see chapter 8 for these). There is also a reference to Paul's epistles to the Laodiceans and to the Alexandrians (these two have not survived) as forgeries to further the teaching of Marcion, commenting, 'it is not fitting that poison should be mixed with honey'.[58] Perhaps the *Muratorian Canon* was in response to the condensed canon of the Gnostic leader Marcion who chose only the Gospel of Luke and ten letters from Paul for his 'canon'. The *Shepherd of Hermas* 'ought to be read' but not alongside the apostles.

This list in the *Muratorian Canon* and the warning against dangerous books, is evidence of the strong stand taken by the early church leaders.

Evidence from the early church leaders to the close of the second century

We have already established that it was not a church council that decided on the books that would form the canon; the churches simply recognized the authorship and authority attached to the various books. This is seen very clearly when we compare what the early leaders said about themselves and their own writings, with what they said about the New Testament books and those who wrote them.

Towards the close of the first century, Clement of Rome wrote a letter to the Christians at Corinth and he clearly had been influenced by the writing of Paul. He makes no claim to apostolic authority, in fact, he writes as a representative of the church at Rome rather than in his own name: 'The Church of God which lives at Rome, to the Church of God living at Corinth.'[59]

Ignatius was the leader in the church at Antioch around the year AD 112, not long after the death of the apostle John. He contrasted himself with

---

57 Through a copyist's error this could be a reference to the epistles of Peter. See Bruce, *The Canon of Scripture*, p.165.
58 *The Muratorian Canon*, Section 3. Translation by F F Bruce.
59 *Epistle of Clement to the Corinthians*, Ch.1:1.

Peter and Paul saying, 'I do not command you, as Peter and Paul did. They were apostles; I am a condemned man.'[60]

Polycarp of Smyrna, possibly the most influential church leader in Asia, tells us that he was a Christian by the year AD 70 and had sat under the teaching of the apostles. Before his martyrdom in AD 155 he referred to himself in this way: 'For neither am I, nor is any other like me, able to follow the wisdom of the blessed and glorious Paul.'[61] He was sure that the apostles wrote with the same authority as the Old Testament prophets: 'Let us therefore so serve Him with fear and all reverence as He himself gave commandment, and the Apostles who preached the Gospel to us, and the prophets who proclaimed beforehand the coming of our Lord.'[62]

Ignatius and Polycarp are typical of the attitude of almost all the early church Fathers.

The first list of New Testament books is found, as we have seen, in the *Muratorian Canon*, compiled somewhere during the mid-second century. However, it would be inaccurate to assume that this was when the New Testament was formed. Although earlier writers do not give us an official list of books, it is quite clear that they knew which books belonged to the body of apostolic authorship, although there is no evidence that any one of them possessed the full canon of twenty-seven books.

One thing is certain: All these early church leaders made a clear distinction between their own writing and the ultimate authority of the apostolic Gospels and letters.

We should remember that these writers were not conscious of the debates that would arise centuries later; they were writing to resolve particular pastoral issues, and what is significant is that in addition to extensive reference to the Old Testament Scriptures, they also made constant use of the Gospels and apostolic writings and expected these to bolster their challenges, warnings and encouragements.[63]

---

60 *Epistle of Ignatius to the Romans*, 4:8–10.
61 *Epistle of Polycarp to the Philippians*, 3:2.
62 As above, 6:5.
63 Metzger, *The Canon of the New Testament*, p. 73, is probably right to suggest that at this stage 'we find the beginning of a movement, unconscious at first' towards accepting the primacy of the words of Jesus preserved in books.

The first three are included here for completeness, but they offer us little information on the development of the canon of the New Testament because they rarely quote from the New Testament. For most of those that follow, more information will be found in chapter 7.

DIDACHE (c. AD 50–80)

Possibly written late in the first century or early in the second, the *Didache* is a short manual of instruction to Christians, and although its existence was known, its content was unknown until a copy was discovered in 1875 in a monastery in Constantinople. The significance is that there are two clear quotations from Matthew's Gospel (6:5ff and 7:6); there are also three other allusions to the same Gospel. Scholars are still divided over whether or not the *Didache* shows any knowledge of the letters of Paul.

EPISTLE OF BARNABAS (c. AD 130)

Though highly regarded among the early churches, Clement of Alexandria and Origen are certainly incorrect in attributing it to the co-worker with Paul, since the destruction of Jerusalem had clearly taken place before it was written. *Barnabas* was of little value, partly because of its extravagant interpretation of the Old Testament. The writer is equally unhelpful in quoting from *The Wisdom of Solomon* and *2 Baruch* as if they are Scripture. However, one value of Barnabas is that in quoting widely from the Old Testament the writer also quotes from the Gospel of Matthew: for example, 'many are called but few are chosen' and he introduces it by 'as it is written'.[64] Similarly, he reveals a clear knowledge of 1 Peter and Romans.[65] There are also echoes, but no more than echoes, of other New Testament books, especially the letters to Timothy.

SHEPHERD OF HERMAS (c. AD 150)

Both the authorship and date of this popular book are uncertain. Nowhere does *Hermas* directly quote from either the Old or New Testaments,

---

64 *The Epistle of Barnabas*, Ch. 4:14.
65 *The Epistle of Barnabas*, Ch. 4:12.

though on many occasions he reveals the influence of canonical books on his thinking, not least the Epistle of James with which he was clearly familiar. *Hermas* also appears to be acquainted with John's Gospel and Ephesians. He almost never quotes from other literature. However, the nature of his writing means that *Hermas* is of little value in assessing what was or was not accepted as canonical in his mind. For the *Shepherd of Hermas* see chapter 7.

PAPIAS OF HIERAPOLIS (AD 69–135 MARTYRED)

Papias must have been alive during the lifetime of those acquainted with the apostles for he concerned himself with the quality, rather than the quantity, of oral traditions and in one preface he wrote:

'I did not, like the multitude, take pleasure in those that speak much, but in those that teach the truth ... If, then, any one came, who had been a follower of the elders, I questioned him in regard to the words of the elders—what Andrew or what Peter said, or what was said by Philip, or by Thomas, or by James, or by John, or by Matthew, or by any other of the disciples of the Lord ... For I did not think that what was to be got from the books would profit me as much as what came from the living and abiding voice.'[66]

Sometimes his sources failed him. For example, Papias heard an odd account of the death of Judas: 'Judas walked about in this world a sad example of impiety; for his body having swollen to such an extent that he could not pass where a chariot could pass easily, he was crushed by the chariot, so that his bowels gushed out'[67]—apparently a case of first century 'Chinese whispers'!

However, Papias does make reference to Matthew 'composing the sayings [of the Lord] in a Hebrew dialect', and he also commented on the Gospel of Mark (John Mark) compiled under the influence of the apostle Peter:

---

66 Papias, *From the Exposition of the Oracles of the Lord*, Ch. 1. We are reliant on the fourth century church historian, Eusebius, for much of our information about Papias. See Eusebius *Ecclesiastical History* Book III, Ch. 39:3–4, *The Writing of Papias*.
67 Papias, *Fragments* III.

'Mark having become the interpreter of Peter, wrote down accurately whatsoever he remembered. It was not, however, in exact order that he related the sayings or deeds of Christ. For he neither heard the Lord nor accompanied Him. But afterwards, as I said, he accompanied Peter, who accommodated his instructions to the necessities [of his hearers], but with no intention of giving a regular narrative of the Lord's sayings. Wherefore Mark made no mistake in thus writing some things as he remembered them. For of one thing he took especial care, not to omit anything he had heard, and not to put anything fictitious into the statements.'[68]

Papias had access both to oral and written records of the life of Christ, even though he appears to have preferred the oral. Elsewhere we learn that Papias was familiar with John's Gospel, 1 Peter, 1 John and Revelation. Whilst there are many New Testament books that Papias does not allude to, we must remember that he is both close to the apostolic age and yet distant from many of the other churches; it is very likely therefore, that Papias had not yet received copies of all the letters of Paul.

IGNATIUS OF ANTIOCH (AD 50–115 MARTYRED)
The leader at Antioch in Syria, and possibly the successor to Peter himself according to some records, wrote seven letters on his journey to Rome where he was martyred. His writing contains many clear references to New Testament books and some scholars claim that he must have known almost the whole of our New Testament—though that claim is possibly a little extravagant. There are few exact quotations because he is writing from memory and under the pressure of travelling as a prisoner, but Ignatius shows that he was acquainted with Matthew's Gospel and particularly quotes from John's Gospel.

Ignatius made wide use of the canonical books. For example, to the Ephesians he commented, 'And you are, as Paul wrote to you, "one body and one spirit, because you have also been called in one hope of the faith. Since also there is one Lord, one faith, one baptism, one God and Father

---

68 Papias, *From the Exposition of the Oracles of the Lord*, Ch. 6. As above, *Ecclesiastical History*, 16.

of all, who is over all, and through all, and in all"'[69]—a quotation from Ephesians 4:4–6.

Ignatius was particularly impressed by Paul's self-effacing comments in 1 Corinthians 15:8–10, and on at least five occasions refers to himself as 'unworthy' or 'the very least'.[70] He wrote to the Magnesians: 'Do your diligence therefore that you be confirmed in the ordinances of the Lord and of the Apostles.'[71] This appears to be a reference to known writings of the Gospels and the epistles.

Nowhere does Ignatius specifically refer to the texts he quotes from as 'Scripture', although he demonstrates a wide knowledge of what we know as canonical books and used only those as his encouragement and authority with the churches.

POLYCARP OF SMYRNA (AD 70–155 MARTYRED)

In Polycarp's letter to the church at Philippi, sometime after AD 110, some scholars have found fifty clear quotations from sixteen New Testament books, including Matthew, Luke, Acts, Romans, 1 Corinthians, Galatians, Ephesians, Philippians, 2 Thessalonians, 1 and 2 Timothy and Hebrews.[72] He quoted accurately from Matthew 7:1–2; 26:41 and Luke 6:36–38 and much more. The absence of some books may simply mean that he had no need to quote from them. Westcott concludes, 'It is wholly unreasonable to doubt that he was acquainted with the chief parts of our Canon.'[73]

Polycarp frequently quoted in a way that implied the Philippians had access to the same written source. He could introduce quotations by: 'Remember what the Lord said in his teaching...' and 'as the Lord has said'.[74] He also referred to 'the commandments of the Lord' and 'the oracles of the Lord',[75] which would have made little sense unless the

---

69 *The Epistle of Ignatius to the Ephesians*, Ch. 6.
70 *Ignatius to the Romans, Ephesians, Traillians, Magnesians and Smyrneans*.
71 *Ignatius to the Magnesians*, 12:8.
72 Westcott says that Polycarp 'contains far more references to the writings of the New Testament than any other work of the first age.' Westcott, *The Canon of the New Testament*, p. 44.
73 Westcott, *The Canon of the New Testament*, p. 44.
74 *The Epistle of Polycarp to the Philippians*, Chs 2 and 7.
75 As above, Ch. 4.

churches had access to written records containing the words of Christ. In each case he quoted accurately from the books as we know them. Among many quotations this could have been taken from either Matthew 26:41 or Mark 14:38: 'as the Lord has said: "The spirit truly is willing, but the flesh is weak."'[76] Polycarp was clearly very familiar with 1 Peter which Bruce Metzger suggests 'he must have known practically by heart'.[77]

Polycarp reveals a wide knowledge of the canonical books, for he quotes and alludes to them often, though without giving his source. It includes a reminder to the Philippians that Paul 'when he was absent, wrote a letter to you',[78] and a quotation from 1 Corinthians 6:2 is attributed to Paul.[79]

Polycarp referred only once to the 'Scriptures' in the context of a New Testament quotation: 'For I trust that you are well versed in the Sacred Scriptures, and that nothing is hid from you ... It is declared then in these Scriptures, "Be ye angry, and sin not" and "Let not the sun go down upon your wrath."'[80] But that single instance is highly significant. It is most natural to assume, in the light of his constant quotations from the New Testament, that it is not merely Ephesians 4:26 that is 'Scripture', but all the quotations he has given.

It is equally significant that although he warmly commends the letters of Ignatius: 'by them you may be greatly profited; for they treat of faith and patience, and all things that tend to edification in our Lord',[81] he never quotes from them to challenge or encourage the Christians as he does with the canonical books.

Polycarp became a Christian in AD 70 and was writing his letter early in the second century; he is therefore one of our earliest witnesses to the growing acceptance of the canonical books.

---

76 As above, Ch. 7.
77 Bruce Metzger, *The Canon of the New Testament*, p. 62.
78 *The Epistle of Polycarp*, Ch. 3.
79 As above, Ch. 11.
80 As above, Ch. 12.
81 As above, Ch. 13.

CLEMENT OF ROME (c. AD 95)

Clement was leader in the church at Rome before the close of the first century and his letter to the church at Corinth, written around AD 95, is of particular interest. He undoubtedly was familiar with Matthew's Gospel, and in his appeal to the church to leave aside its schism, Clement referred to Matthew 18:6–7, though without attributing his source but in such a way that assumes they have access to it:

'Remember the words of our Lord Jesus Christ, how He said, "Woe to that man. It were better for him that he had never been born, than that he should cast a stumbling-block before one of my elect. Yes, it were better for him that a millstone should be hung about him, and he should be sunk in the depths of the sea, than that he should cast a stumbling-block before one of my little ones.'[82]

Clement did not feel obliged to quote exactly, and he therefore adds phrases that do not belong in Matthew 18. Perhaps Mark 14:19 and Matthew 24:24 are in his mind. However, he was more specific when it came to Paul's letters. Clement was well aware that Paul had written to Corinth on the same issues, and he assumed that the church possessed a copy and that they would accept that it was written under the inspiration of the Spirit:

'Take up the epistle of the blessed Apostle Paul. What did he write to you at the time when the Gospel first began to be preached? Truly, under the inspiration of the Spirit, he wrote to you concerning himself, and Cephas, and Apollos...'[83]

That phrase 'under the inspiration of the Spirit' (literally 'spiritually' or 'in the Spirit') is a clear indication that the churches not only possessed Paul's letter to the Corinthians, but that they attributed to it divine authorship. The way Clement writes here implies that already the churches were gathering apostolic letters that they could refer to as authoritative. Similarly, Clement quoted from Psalm 118:18 and Hebrews 12:6 (though without giving either source) and described both as the 'Holy Word'.[84]

---

82 *Clement of Rome to the Corinthians*, 46.
83 As above, 47.
84 As above, 56.

In all, Clement reveals a knowledge (either by quotation or allusion) of at least one of the Gospels as well as Hebrews, Romans, Acts, Galatians, Ephesians, Philippians, 1 Timothy, Titus, 1 Peter and James. Remember, Clement was writing before the turn of the first century. However, whilst he repeatedly introduces his Old Testament references as 'Scripture' he does not do the same with his quotations or paraphrases from what became New Testament books. On the other hand, Clement uses them equally with the Old Testament to enforce his arguments, and considered Hebrews to be the 'Holy Word' and Paul to have written under the guidance of the Spirit.

THE SECOND EPISTLE OF CLEMENT (c. AD 150?)

This was not written by Clement of Rome and may be the text of an early Christian sermon.[85] Probably dated around AD 150, the author is unknown. The writer is clearly familiar with Matthew and Luke and at times combines quotations from each. Frequently he introduces his quotations by 'the Lord says'. He was also familiar with 1 Corinthians and Ephesians. There is a hint of Gnostic ideas occasionally, and this is probably why the epistle was not widely circulated.

Significantly this epistle quoted from Isaiah 56 and added, 'and another Scripture however says, "I did not come to call the righteous but sinners."' This quotation comes from Matthew 9:13.[86] This is an unusually explicit identification at this period and although the epistle cannot be highly regarded, it does imply that the move towards positively equating the Gospels and apostolic writing with Scripture, was already under way by the mid-second century. Paul and Peter had made the same identification: Paul in 1 Timothy 5:18 introducing both Deuteronomy 25:4 and Luke 10:7 as 'the Scripture says', and Peter in 2 Peter 3:16 linking Paul's letters with 'the other Scriptures').

---

85 So Metzger, The Canon of the New Testament, p. 67.
86 The Second Epistle of Clement: 2:7–8. Though not from Clement, some date it as early as AD 98–100.

JUSTIN OF ROME (AD 110–165 MARTYRED)

Justin was one of the first and most capable of the Christian apologists who defended the faith to the Emperor Antoninus Pius and the Roman Senate. He does not quote by name from any New Testament writing, but he frequently used the four Gospels and employed the formulae of quotation 'it is recorded' and 'it is written', when quoting from the 'Memoirs of the apostles' or simply the 'Memoirs'. These memoirs, Justin tells his non-Christian readers, were called the 'Gospels'. In his first apology to Trypho the Jew, he quoted widely and accurately from the Gospel of Matthew in particular.

We have seen how, for the benefit of the emperor, Justin outlined the Christian Sunday services of worship during which, 'The memoirs of the apostles or the writings of the prophets are read...'[87] Interestingly, the apostles are here placed in front of the prophets, and it is clearly assumed that the churches possessed, if not a complete, yet a significant collection of those 'memoirs'.

Justin was careful to distinguish those Gospels that were written by an apostle (Matthew and John) and those under the influence of an apostle (Mark and Luke). When he referred to Mark 3:16 (the name change of Peter), he referred to this Gospel as Peter's, which means that he followed the view of Papias that Peter was the apostle behind Mark's Gospel.[88] Similarly, when Justin quoted from Luke 22:42,44 (Luke was not an apostle) he noted, 'in the memoirs which I say were drawn up by His apostles and those who followed them, [it is recorded] that His sweat fell down like drops of blood while He was praying, and saying, 'If it be possible, let this cup pass.'[89]

Occasionally Justin added a phrase or two to the Gospel text, but this does not necessarily mean that he had access to 'non-canonical' sources; perhaps he was simply elaborating as any preacher might. Only twice he offered two brief quotations from Jesus that are not found in the four Gospels.

---

87 Justin's first *Apology*, Ch. 67.
88 *Justin to Trypho*, Ch. 106.
89 As above, Ch. 103.

In his long letter to the Jew Trypho, Justin made a clear reference to the book of Revelation and, whilst he did not quote from Paul, it would seem certain that he was familiar with the apostle's writing. He gave equal authority to the writings of the Gospels and apostles as he did to the Old Testament. It is common for Justin to introduce New Testament quotations by the phrase 'It is written'; for example when quoting Matthew 17:13 he wrote, 'And it is written, "Then the disciples understood that He spoke to them about John the Baptist."'[90]

Justin's many references to the Gospels and apostles are often rough paraphrases rather than precise and accurate quotations; though there are many exceptions to this.[91] However, Bishop Westcott offers the interesting explanation that this actually indicates his familiarity with the text—he was so familiar with the sources that he did not bother to check the accuracy.[92] Justin was just as lax in quoting from the Old Testament and from secular writers.

TATIAN OF ROME AND SYRIA (AD 110–180)

We know little about Tatian except that, according to the early Christian historian Eusebius, he was converted under Justin Martyr in Rome and later wrote a number of books in the middle of the second century, only one of which has survived. We do know that he compiled a harmony of the four Gospels, and this is known as Tatian's *Diatessaron*—borrowed from the language of music meaning literally 'through the four'. Only a fragment of this has survived, discovered in Syria as recently as 1933. It has the distinction of being the only New Testament document dated before the fourth century to be discovered outside Egypt—with the possible exception of 7Q5 (see Book 4 chapter 3 in this series).

The *Diatessaron* is important evidence to show that the four Gospels were in use and regarded as authoritative Scripture well before AD 150. Some of the false gospels (for which see chapter 8) may have been circulating by this time and yet Tatian ignored them all in preference for

---

90 As above, Ch.49.
91 Justin's first *Apology*. See Chs 15 to 17 in particular.
92 B F Westcott, *The Canon of the New Testament*, p.141.

the four Gospels. This is true of all the leaders during the second century whose records show that they used only the four. The *Diatessaron* was very popular, particularly in Syria.

Unfortunately, this clear acceptance of the four Gospels by Tatian was not followed by a full acceptance of the letters of Paul: he rejected some, because they did not agree with his own strict practice which included abstaining from meat, wine and marriage. However, Tatian was clearly aware of many other epistles and used them positively.

DIONYSIUS OF CORINTH (c. AD 165)

Regrettably, we have only fragments of the helpful letters that Dionysius wrote to several churches in the middle of the second century, but he offers a significant comment that the heretics ('apostles of the devil') had taken his letters and changed and twisted them ('taking away some things and adding others'); he concluded, 'It is, therefore, not to be wondered at if some have attempted to adulterate the Scriptures ('writings') of the Lord also, since they have formed designs even against writings which are of less accounts.'[93]

Dionysius wrote firmly against the Gnostics; Marcion in particular was probably guilty of interfering with the texts of the apostles. Dionysius is clear that what he writes is 'of less account' than those that carry the authority of the Lord himself. Obviously he expected his readers to agree with this high view of the Gospels and apostles.

ARISTIDES (c. AD 126) AND ATHENAGORAS (c. AD 133–190) OF ATHENS

Aristides wrote his *Apology* somewhere around AD 126 and addressed it to the Emperor Hadrian. He does not quote from the New Testament books, though his language at times is clearly influenced by the epistles, and in one significant phrase he directs the emperor to a book of the Gospel that the emperor could read for himself if he wished: 'This is taught in the gospel, as it is called, which a short time was preached among them; and you also if you will read therein, may perceive the power which belongs to it.'[94]

---

93 Eusebius, *Ecclesiastical History*, Book IV. Ch. 23:12.
94 Aristides, *Apology*, Ch. 2.

Towards the end he declares: 'Take, then, their [Christian] writings, and read therein, and lo! you will find that I have not put forth these things on my own authority.'[95] It is tempting to speculate that a copy of that Gospel may have accompanied this appeal.

Athenagoras wrote *A Plea for the Christians* to the Emperor Marcus Aurelius around AD 170. This brief but able defence of the faith was not too dissimilar from that of Aristides which he may well have had access to. He uses both the Old Testament books and the Gospels and epistles sparingly, but there are references to Matthew, Mark and John and at least Romans, Galatians and 1 Timothy; this does not mean he was ignorant of more. To the mind of Athenagoras, writing to a pagan emperor it was unnecessary to use Scripture as his authority, and he wields instead the pagan philosophers and poets to demolish what he sees as the absurdity of polytheism.

SUMMARY UP TO AD 180

Well before the middle of the second century, many leaders of the churches possessed a significant body of New Testament Gospels and letters, and expected the churches to have the same. They quoted these, and only these, as having an authority equal to that of the Old Testament.[96] The agreement of theology found in their writings, is evidence of a common use of the four Gospels and the letters of the apostles.[97]

---

95 Aristides, *Apology*, Ch.16.
96 Westcott concludes: 'Scarcely a fragment of the earliest Christian literature had been preserved which does not contain some passing allusion to the Apostolic writing; and yet in all there is no discrepancy. The influence of some common rule is the only natural explanation of this common consent.' *The Canon of the New Testament*, pp. 365,368.
97 Westcott, *The Canon of the New Testament*, 'The form of Christian doctrine current throughout the church, as represented by men most widely differing in national and personal characteristics, in books of the most varied aim and composition, is measured exactly by the Apostolic Canon.' p. 250. In other words: the theology of all these early writers agrees with the New Testament.

5. A complete New Testament

From the second half of the second century there was an increasing use of New Testament books in the writing of the church leaders.

Spurred by the urgent need to instruct the young Christians in the face of growing persecution and the onslaught of the heretics, it was inevitable that there would be an increased awareness of the authority that underpinned the Christian faith. By the middle of the second century, at least twenty-two of the New Testament books were acknowledged as apostolic and authoritative throughout the churches across the Roman empire, even though, apart from the *Muratorian Canon*, no formal canonical list had been compiled.

Irenaeus and Tertullian form a bridge between the two centuries, but in considering the evidence of these two giants and others, we must never forget that they were fallible men whose theology in other areas was sometimes less than exact. Tertullian later became a Montanist and Origen, though thoroughly Trinitarian in his theology, was too much influenced by the Greek philosopher Plato.

THE SCILITAN MARTYRS

On 17 July 180, seven men and five women were executed by the proconsul Saturninus in Carthage. They refused to worship the emperor and had in their possession what they referred to as: 'Our customary books, and the epistles of Paul, a devout man...' Here in North Africa, a group of ordinary Christians were carrying with them a collection of books which included the epistles of Paul.

IRENAEUS OF LYONS (AD 130–202)

Irenaeus, who had been a student under Polycarp, wrote five large books *Against Heresies* around AD 180.[98] The 'heretics' chiefly in his sights were the Gnostics, who dispensed with the Old Testament and were very selective over which books from the new order they would accept. (See chapter 8 for more on the Gnostics and how Irenaeus dealt with them.) This compelled Irenaeus to declare his hand and make clear which books were generally accepted as carrying apostolic authority equal to that of the prophets in the Old Testament. His use of accepted books is therefore valuable. Irenaeus had contacts across the Roman world and was well placed to speak for the churches as a whole.

In *Against Heresies*, Irenaeus quoted from over one thousand passages covering most of the New Testament. This included all of Paul's epistles with the exception of Philemon. The book of Revelation was clearly one of his favourites. The exceptions are Philemon, 3 John and possibly also James, 2 Peter, Hebrews and Jude—although this does not mean he did not know of them or did not accept them. He had no doubt that the Gospels and apostles were 'Holy Scripture'.[99]

For Irenaeus, the four Gospels, and none other, were the only accepted testament to the life of Christ:

'It is not possible that the Gospels can be either more or fewer in number than they are. For, since there are four zones of the world in which we live, and four principal winds, while the Church is scattered throughout all the world, and the "pillar and ground" of the Church is the Gospel and the spirit of life, it is fitting that she should have four pillars, breathing out immortality on every side, and vivifying men afresh...'[100]

Irenaeus commented that even the heretics use the Gospels, whilst twisting them to their own ends: 'So firm is the ground upon which these Gospels rest, that the very heretics themselves bear witness to them, and,

---

98   His title was, An Exposure and Refutation of the Knowledge *(gnosis) that is Falsely So Called*.
99   Irenaeus, *Against Heresies*. For example, in Book III, Ch.17:4 Irenaeus refers to 'Texts of Holy Scripture used by these heretics to support their opinions', which reveals Irenaeus' clear acceptance of the Gospels and the apostles as 'Holy Scripture'.
100 As above, Book III, Ch.11:8.

starting from these [documents], each one of them endeavours to establish his own peculiar doctrine.'[101]

Irenaeus gave the Acts of the Apostles equal status with the Gospels and, following Papias, Irenaeus believed Mark was the 'disciple and interpreter of Peter'.[102] Against the heretics and their spurious writings, Irenaeus insisted that the true faith came through the apostles who handed it down in writing:

'We have learned from none others the plan of our salvation than from those through whom the Gospel has come down to us, which they did at one time proclaim in public, and, at a later period, by the will of God, handed down to us in the Scriptures, to be the ground and pillar of our faith.'[103]

Irenaeus continued that they were 'invested with power from on high when the Holy Spirit came down' so that they might have 'perfect knowledge'—that phrase was a certain dig at the Gnostics and their boasted wisdom and secret knowledge.

Irenaeus had no doubt that God was the author of both the Old Testament and the four Gospels and the New Testament letters. They are all clearly labelled 'Scripture' in his writing. For him, a book was canonical if it was written by or under the authority of an apostle, and that the churches generally had accepted it. On this basis, Irenaeus possessed a canon of New Testament books almost identical to ours—and that in the year 180.

Irenaeus was impressed by the unbroken line of Christian leaders from the apostle Paul who had carefully passed on the truth: 'This is most abundant proof that there is one and the same vivifying faith, which has been preserved in the Church from the apostles until now, and handed down in truth.'[104] Although he never provided his readers with a list of accepted books in the New Testament canon, he must have had such a list in his mind since, with the single exception of the *Shepherd of Hermas*,

---

101 As above, Book III, Ch.11:7.
102 As above, Book III, Ch.1:1.
103 As above.
104 As above, Book III, Ch.3:3.

he only ever used the canonical books for his authority in rebuffing the heretics. With the addition of 1 Peter, the books used by Irenaeus are the same as those in the *Muratorian Canon* to which he may have had access.[105]

TERTULLIAN OF CARTHAGE (AD 155–220)

Perhaps the greatest theologian of the second century, and a formidable opponent of the Gnostic heretics, was born in Carthage. Tertullian was a highly educated African who became a lawyer and moved to Rome where he was converted around AD 195. He later returned to his home town. At the turn of the century he joined the Montanists, a group of early Pentecostalists, and died sometime after AD 220.

Tertullian undoubtedly speaks not only for the African church, but for the church at large, and he complements the work of Irenaeus and takes the evidence for the canon a stage further. He allowed no distinction between the law, the prophets and the apostles; together they formed the rule of faith:

'The apostolic churches, in which the very thrones of the apostles are still pre-eminent in their places, in which their own authentic writings are read ... the law and the prophets she unites in one volume with the writings of evangelists and apostles, from which she drinks in her faith.'[106]

Further:

'We lay it down as our first position, that the evangelical Testament has apostles for its authors, to whom was assigned by the Lord Himself this office of publishing the gospel ... Of the apostles, therefore, John and Matthew first instil faith into us; whilst of apostolic men, Luke and Mark renew it afterwards.'[107]

When he wrote of 'the records of the faith'[108] there can be little doubt that Tertullian had a recognized collection of books in mind, and he carefully distinguished between the apostles (Matthew and John) and

---

105 So F F Bruce, *The Canon of Scripture* (InterVarsity Press, Illinois 1988), p.177.
106 Tertullian, *The Prescription Against Heretics*, Ch. 36.
107 Tertullian, *Against Marcion*, Book IV, Ch. 2.
108 Tertullian, *The Prescription Against Heresies*, Ch.14.

'apostolic men' (Mark and Luke). Tertullian wrote at length about the apostles; for example: 'In the Lord's apostles we possess our authority, for even they did not of themselves choose to introduce anything, but faithfully delivered to the nations the doctrine which they have received from Christ.' [109] He used the phrase 'New Testament' to refer to the second part of the Christian Bible.

Tertullian considered Barnabas to be the author of Hebrews,[110] however, that made no difference to its authority since Barnabas was a close companion of the apostle Paul. Significantly, Tertullian did not accept the *Shepherd of Hermas* and claimed that it has been widely rejected by the churches—he called it 'The apocryphal "Shepherd" of adulterers.' [111]

As a lawyer, we are not surprised at his preference for the written word—what he refers to as 'the majesty of our Scriptures'.[112] In one of his works Tertullian wrote, 'But let us rather be mindful of the sayings of the Lord, and of the letters of the apostles; for they have both told us beforehand that there shall be heresies, and have given us, in anticipation, warnings to avoid them.' [113]

No longer do we have scattered quotations or allusions to New Testament books; Tertullian is perhaps the first serious expositor. Typical of his handling of Scripture is when he turned his attention to Paul's letter to the Galatians. He set himself to analyse the very words that Paul used:

'The epistle which we also allow to be the most decisive against Judaism, is that wherein the apostle instructs the Galatians.... It is clear enough in what sense he writes, "I marvel that you are so soon removed from Him who has called you to His grace to *another* gospel"—He means "another" as to the conduct it prescribes, not in respect of its worship; "another" as to the discipline it teaches, not in respect of its divinity.' [114]

---

109 Tertullian, *The Prescription Against Heretics*, Ch. 6.
110 Tertullian on *Modesty*, Ch. 20.
111 As above.
112 Tertullian, *Apologetic*, Ch. 20.
113 Tertullian, *The Prescription Against Heretics*, Ch. 4.
114 Tertullian, *Against Marcion*, Book V, Ch. 2.

In his defence of the true faith—what he referred to as 'the rule of faith' (*regula fidei*)—Tertullian used all the New Testament books except James, 2 and 3 John and 2 Peter; of Paul's letters, only Philemon is missing. He simply had no need to use these. Tertullian quoted from Revelation frequently, and ascribed it to John. There can be no doubt that he possessed a collection of books that he recognised as the regulators of faith, and it was likely to be almost, if not wholly, identical to our canon of the New Testament. It is also evident from Tertullian that the Gospels and apostolic letters had already been translated from the Greek into Latin by his day. Tertullian was aware that Irenaeus had already made such translations. This, at the turn of the second century.

CYPRIAN OF CARTHAGE (AD 210–258 MARTYRED)

Born shortly after AD 200, Cyprian was converted around AD 246, sold all his property for the poor and vowed chastity and poverty. He became a keen student of Scripture and of Tertullian. His brilliant mind meant that he was appointed bishop of Carthage, the leading church in North Africa. Cyprian was a prolific writer, and much of his work has survived. He recognised only the four Gospels and one scholar has computed that he quoted in his letters from almost ten percent of the New Testament.[115] He does not quote from Philemon, Hebrews, James, 2 Peter, 2 and 3 John and Jude. He must have known Hebrews because Tertullian used it frequently and there is at least one clear allusion to it.[116] All his quotations are prefaced with 'it is written' or 'Scriptures' or something similar.

HIPPOLYTUS OF ROME (AD 170–235 MARTYRED)

We know little about the early life of Hippolytus except that he was born around AD 170 and studied under Irenaeus. On moving to Rome, he soon established his reputation as a preacher and writer and is considered the greatest Christian scholar in the West at this time.

---

115 Metzger, *The Canon of the New Testament*, citing the work of von Soden (Leipzig 1909).
116 Cyprian, *On the Lord's Prayer*. 1. Clearly the influence of Hebrews 1:1–2.

Writing between AD 200 and his death, he has more than forty works to his name, including commentaries on Scripture and Christian doctrine. He wrote ten books on *A Refutation of all Heresies*. Unfortunately, little has survived, but it appears that his 'canon' was almost identical to the *Muratorian Canon*.[117] Hippolytus accepted only the four Gospels as records of the life and ministry of Christ, plus thirteen letters of Paul, Acts and 1 Peter and 1 and 2 John and the Apocalypse of John. He often quoted from Hebrews, though did not equate it with Scripture. There is little doubt that those books he did accept were placed on the same level with Old Testament texts. He quoted from other books, such as the *Shepherd of Hermas* and *Didache*, but never with the same authority as the canonical literature which he introduced by such expressions as 'the Lord says' and 'the apostle says'. He was aware of 2 Peter, though did not recognise it as Scripture.

CLEMENT OF ALEXANDRIA (AD 153–216)

Clement arrived in Alexandria around AD 180 and ten years later was leader of the theological training school there until he was forced into exile under the severe persecution of the Emperor Severus. Clement was a skilful warrior against the Gnostics. In his lengthy and detailed writings, he quoted from the New Testament books almost twice as often as from the Old Testament, and according to one source his total number of references to the Gospels and Paul amount to almost 3,000.[118] Writing on faith, Clement referred to 'the precepts both of the Old and of the New Testament'.[119] Tertullian may have been the first to refer to 'The New Testament',[120] but at least it shows that the phrase was now becoming familiar, and it implies a known group of books.

---

117 See Bruce Metzger, *The Canon of the New Testament*, p.150. Though Metzger does not necessarily subscribe to this view. Hippolytus was the last of the great leaders in the West to use Greek as his language of writing.
118 As above, pp.131,133–134. Quoting the work of Otto Stählin.
119 Clement of Alexandria, *Stromata* (Miscellanies), Book 1, Ch.1.
120 So F F Bruce, *The Canon of Scripture*, p.180.

Clement quoted from all the New Testament books with the exception of Philemon, James, 2 Peter and 2 and 3 John, which he probably had no need to refer to. He followed others in accepting that Hebrews was penned by the apostle Paul.[121] In his *Exhortation to the Heathen* he quotes from Matthew, Romans, Corinthians, Galatians, Ephesians, Hebrews and Timothy.

Clement accepted only the four Gospels and insisted that they were entirely in harmony with each other. He was aware of a few other 'gospels', but he was careful always to distinguish them from the four and never allowed them the same authority. Clement was prepared to use the title 'Scripture' when quoting from the Gospels; for example at Matthew 23:37: 'The Scripture testifies: "As a hen gathers her chickens under her wings." Thus are we the Lord's chickens; the Word thus marvellously and mystically describing the simplicity of childhood.'[122]

Whilst Clement is hesitant on some New Testament books, his 'canon' was fairly well defined in his own mind. He united the Old and New Testament books in a vivid musical metaphor: 'the ecclesiastical symphony at once of the law and the prophets, and the apostles along with the Gospel'.[123]

However, Eusebius claimed that Clement was using all the New Testament books 'without omitting the disputed books'—which means that Clement was prepared to use books in addition to those accepted by apostolic authority. He appears also to have included *Barnabas* and the so-called *Revelation of Peter* among these.

ORIGEN OF ALEXANDRIA (AD 180–253)
Almost certainly a student of Clement, and as a theologian and biblical scholar, Origen towered above most of his contemporaries. One Professor of New Testament Greek referred to him, perhaps somewhat over generously, as: 'The greatest biblical scholar who ever lived.'[124]

121 Eusebius, *Ecclesiastical History*, VI.14.
122 Clement of Alexandria, *Instructor*, Ch. 5.
123 Clement of Alexandria, *Stromata*, Book VI, Ch. 11.
124 Alexander Souter, *The Canon of the New Testament*. (Duckworth & Co., London 1913), p.174.

Born in Egypt, Origen travelled widely as a teacher before, at the age of eighteen, succeeding Clement as head of the catechetical (training) school in Alexandria. For twelve years he worked hard and successfully until the bitter persecution under Caracalla forced him into temporary exile at Caesarea before he returned to Alexandria.

Sadly, unnecessary church wrangling over his ordination forced him back to Caesarea where he opened a new school which was even more successful than that at Alexandria. In AD 250 under the persecution of Decian, he was tortured and condemned. Only the death of the emperor saved him from burning; however, his health had been broken and Origen died soon after in AD 253.

As a skilful biblical expositor, it is claimed that he expounded almost all the books of the Old and New Testaments. Although much of his work is lost, there is still a valuable collection. Origen had travelled widely in Egypt, Arabia, Asia Minor, Greece, Rome and Palestine, and therefore he knew which books of the New Testament canon were accepted by which churches. No one in his day had a more accurate knowledge of this subject. Origen followed Clement in referring to 'The New Testament' and unequivocally identified them with the Old Testament books: 'This just and good God, the Father of our Lord Jesus Christ, Himself gave the law and the prophets, and the Gospels, being also the God of the apostles and of the Old and New Testaments.' [125]

Origen had no doubt that the writings of the apostles were 'Scripture'. After quoting at length from Romans, for example, he continued, 'You will find also innumerable other passages in holy Scripture.' [126] He went further, and reflected the view 'throughout the churches' when he wrote of the Scriptures, both Old and New Testaments, as inspired by the Spirit:

'[The] Spirit inspired each one of the saints, whether prophets or apostles; and that there was not one Spirit in the men of the old dispensation, and another in those who were inspired at the advent of Christ, is most clearly taught throughout the

---

125 Origen, *De Principiis* (*Concerning Principles*), Preface 4. He used the title 'New Testament' six times in *De Principiis*.
126 Origen, *De Principiis*, Ch.1:6.

Churches ... Those Scriptures alone which were inspired by the Holy Spirit, i.e. the Gospels and Epistles, and the law and the prophets, according to the declaration of Christ Himself.'[127]

Origen maintained that the four Gospels were 'the only indisputable ones in the church of God under heaven', and he went on to list some of the false gospels that are rejected, stating that he had read them all to check their value.[128] He admitted that Peter's second epistle was disputed by some, and a few even tried to reject Paul's second letter to Timothy 'but they were not able.' He had no doubt that Luke wrote both the Gospel and Acts, and that John wrote both his Gospel and the Apocalypse. Hebrews, from which he quoted on more than two hundred occasions, he attributed to the apostle Paul, though admitting that its authorship is uncertain: 'Who wrote the epistle, in truth, God knows.'

Origen occasionally quoted from other, non-canonical books, though without attributing the same authority to them. He quoted from Clement of Rome, the *Epistle of Barnabas*, and the *Shepherd of Hermas*—which he even once suggests might be 'divinely inspired'. However, none of this detracts from the fact that it was only 'canonical' books that formed the basis of his many expository addresses. The only New Testament books that Origen did not use (although he accepted them), in his writings are 2 Peter and 2 and 3 John and he acknowledged that these, together with James, Jude and Hebrews, are disputed by some churches, although he did not share these doubts. In a later work, written around AD 240, Origen summarised much of the New Testament canon in a graphic style. The four Gospels:

'each gave forth a strain on their priestly trumpets. Peter, moreover, sounds with the two trumpets of his epistles ... Last of all thundering on the fourteen trumpets of his epistles he [Paul] threw down, even to their very foundations, the walls of Jericho, that is to say, all the instruments of idolatry and the dogmas of the philosophers.'[129]

---

127 Origen, *De Principiis*, Preface 4 and Ch. 3:1.
128 Eusebius in *Ecclesiastical History* VI, Ch. 35:4.
129 Origen, *Homilies in Jos*, VII.1.

EUSEBIUS OF CAESAREA (AD 260–340)

Eusebius was the first church historian, leader in the church at Caesarea from AD 313 and a close advisor to the Emperor Constantine after Constantine's acceptance of the Christian faith. By this time a library of Christian writings of significant historical value had been gathered at Caesarea, and Eusebius was able to make full use of it. His *Ecclesiastical History* (from the birth of Christ to AD 313) is one of the most valuable books from that period, since Eusebius had read many authors and had also travelled widely.

Eusebius claimed that he had enquired into the view of all the churches concerning the accepted books of Scripture, and he had searched widely.[130] There is no evidence that he was acting on the instructions of a church, council or the emperor. His research was the result of his personal desire to discover the truth. He admitted that there was no one official list of canonical books, so he made his own from what books the various churches were using.

Eusebius drew up three lists:

- *The recognised books:* those universally accepted by the churches. Under this category Eusebius listed the four Gospels, Acts, the fourteen letters of Paul (including Hebrews), 1 Peter, 1 John and the Apocalypse of John. That is, twenty-two books that the churches accepted without question. Eusebius does, however, acknowledge that some disputed the authorship of Hebrews.[131]

- *The disputed books:* those that some accepted and others queried or rejected. These were James, Jude, 2 Peter and 2 and 3 John. Though they are known to most of the churches—the implication of this

---

130 An intriguing comment by Eusebius (*Ecclesiastical History*, Book V, Ch. 10) refers to Pantaenus a teacher of Clement in Alexandria 'a man highly distinguished for his learning' who 'is said to have gone to India. It is reported that among persons there who knew of Christ, he found the Gospel according to Matthew, which had anticipated his own arrival. For Bartholomew, one of the apostles, had preached to them, and left with them the writing of Matthew in the Hebrew language, which they had preserved till that time.' It is impossible to verify this account.

131 Eusebius, *Ecclesiastical History*. For his full lists: Book III, 25 and following.

being that some churches simply may not have yet received copies of these books.

- *The rejected books:* those that all churches considered spurious and these included the *Acts of Paul,* the *Shepherd of Hermas,* the *Acts of Peter,* the *Apocalypse of Peter,* the *Epistle of Barnabas,* and the *Gospel According to the Hebrews.* These were a few of the heretical or pseudepigraphal writings. Even worse than these books, in the mind of Eusebius are such heretical books that pretend to come from an apostle such as the Gospels of Peter, Thomas, Matthias and others.

Given the widespread and independent nature of the churches and the heavy hand of persecution that frequently robbed the churches of their leaders, the catalogue of Eusebius showed a remarkable degree of unanimity. For his own part, Eusebius accepted all except James, 2 Peter and Jude, though he admitted that they were widely used among the churches.

His list is not quite as tidy as the foregoing appears, because occasionally he placed the same book in two lists; the Apocalypse of John for example. However, Metzger provides a reasonable explanation for this in that Eusebius, writing as the historian, acknowledged that it was widely accepted among the churches, but for his own part he was exasperated by the extravagant use some were making of the Apocalypse and thus questioned its validity.[132]

In AD 332 Eusebius was ordered by the Emperor Constantine to prepare fifty expertly inscribed copies of the Scriptures at the imperial expense. Eusebius carried out his orders and the books were presented to the Emperor for safe keeping. Since none of these books has yet been identified, we do not know what canon was included in that New Testament. Some consider that *Codex Sinaiticus* and/or *Codex Vaticanus* may have been one of those fifty copies. (See in this series Book 4 chapter 3.) This is impossible to judge now, but they are both of the same time as Eusebius and their canon of books is identical to ours, with

---

132 Metzger, *The Canon of the New Testament,* p. 205.

the addition of *Barnabas* and *Hermas* added to the end of *Sinaiticus*, both of which Eusebius rejected.

There can be little reasonable doubt that by this time—in the first quarter of the fourth century—the canon was almost universally fixed. Westcott concludes also, with a little exaggeration, that the apocryphal writings 'had passed almost out of notice'.[133]

ATHANASIUS OF ALEXANDRIA (AD 296–373)

Athanasius was undoubtedly the most well-known theologian of the fourth century. Born around AD 296 he was educated in his home city of Alexandria, and at the Council of Nicea in AD 325 Athanasius took a leading role in the battle against Arius who denied the true deity of Christ. Soon after accepting leadership of the church at Alexandria, he took advantage of his position to set out the acknowledged limits of the New Testament canon.

In his *Festal Epistle* for the year 367, Athanasius listed the entire canon, both Old and New Testaments exactly as we have it today (though Esther is missing from the Old Testament list but added as a useful book). The order of books varies, and Hebrews comes before 1 Timothy—an indication that Athanasius believed Hebrews belonged to Paul. Athanasius therefore provides the first list of New Testament books exactly as we have them; the few doubts of Eusebius are evidently not shared by Athanasius. This is particularly significant because of the many apocryphal books that were circulating among the Egyptians who seemed to have a special fondness for heretical works.

Here are his own words:

'As the heretics are quoting apocryphal writings, an evil which was rife even as early as when St. Luke wrote his gospel, therefore I have thought good to set forth clearly what books have been received by us through tradition as belonging to the Canon, and which we believe to be divine. [Then follows the books of the Old Testament with the unusual addition of the Epistle of Baruch]. Of the New Testament these are the books ... [then follows the twenty-seven books of our New Testament, and no

---

133 Westcott, *The Canon of the New Testament*, pp. 467–468.

more] ... These are the fountains of salvation, that whoever thirsts, may be satisfied by the eloquence which is in them. In them alone is set forth the doctrine of piety. Let no one add to them, nor take anything from them.' [134]

Athanasius was the first to use the word 'canon' to refer to the collection of New Testament books, adding for further accuracy:

'that there are certain other books, not edited in the Canon, but established by the Fathers, to be read by those who have just come to us and wish to be instructed in the doctrine of piety. The *Wisdom of Solomon*, the *Wisdom of Sirach*, *Esther*, *Judith*, *Tobit*, the *Doctrine of the Apostles* [the *Didache*] and the *Pastor* [the *Shepherd of Hermas*]. And let none of the apocrypha of the heretics be read among you.'

JEROME OF ROME (AD 347–420) AND AUGUSTINE OF HIPPO (AD 354–430)

If we could stop with Athanasius, the picture would be relatively neat and complete. However, the history of the canon does not quite end there in the year AD 367. Various leaders from different parts of the rapidly crumbling Roman empire revealed the extent of their own canon: Gregory of Nazianzus, Amphilochius of Iconium, Didymus the Blind in Alexandria, Epiphanius of Salamis (Cyprus), John Chrysostom in Antioch and later Constantinople (perhaps the first to use the word 'Bible' to refer to the complete collection of Old and New Testaments), Theodore of Mopsuestia (Cilicia) and Theodoret of Cyrrhus.

There are differences to a small extent between them, but the conclusion is this: among them all, the canonical books as we know them were universally accepted and on only five books were any serious questions raised: 2 Peter, 2 and 3 John, Jude and Revelation. The latter, largely because of the abuse made from it by the millenarians, with their extreme views of the second coming. [135]

---

134 From the *Festal Epistle* of Athanasius XXXIX. Translated in *Nicene and Post-Nicene Fathers*, Vol. IV, pp. 551,552.
135 For the detail of some of these later writers see Metzger, *The Canon of the New Testament*, pp. 212–217. And Bruce, *The Canon of Scripture*.

The position in the Western churches is not too dissimilar. There are eccentricities to be sure, but the general pattern is clear, and Tyrannius Rufinus who was born in AD 345, well reflects the churches in the West. His canon was the same as that of Athanasius (except that the order differed) and he listed additional books that were useful but not canonical, and those 'that should not be read out in church.'

Jerome (Eusebius Hieronymus), born around the same time as Rufinus, adopted the same canon for his Latin 'Vulgate', as did Augustine. Whilst Jerome himself entertained no doubts about the twenty-seven books, he listed the queries raised by some parts of the church. He was probably the first to suggest, in defence of 2 Peter, that the difference in style and Greek usage was probably due to different scribes who, at Peter's dictation, converted his Galilean Aramaic into Greek.[136] For Jerome the canon was fixed.

Augustine was present at the Synods of Hippo (AD 393), and Carthage (397 and again in 419) at which the canon of twenty-seven books that we know, was recognised as the one in use universally among the western churches.[137] Whilst accepting the canon that he received, identical to that of Athanasius, though with a slightly changed order, Augustine was not afraid to ask the pertinent question: 'Why these and no others?' His answer was, like Jerome, not dependant solely on proving apostolic authorship. Instead: First, those with universal acceptance should be accepted without further judgement. Second, those over which some churches expressed doubts should be accepted according to the majority of churches and the authority of their leaders.[138]

At this time, no council of leaders had attempted to pronounce on the canon on behalf of all the churches.

Inevitably, with Christian churches scattered well beyond the frontiers of the Roman Empire, and with no one church as 'supremo' above all the others, here and there the canon was ragged at the edges. But for all

---

136 Jerome, *Letter to Hedeba*, 406–7.
137 Augustine's list can be found in *Of The Doctrine of Christ*, Book II, 12:8. It agrees exactly with our Canon.
138 Augustine, *On Christian Learning*, 2:12.

practical purposes, this marks the terminus of the debate on the canon of the New Testament. At the time of the Reformation, Erasmus (a Roman Catholic) and Luther (a Protestant Reformer) made their own individual observations on canonical books over which they held personal doubts. Tyndale followed Luther in placing Hebrews (which Tyndale calls 'the epistle of Paul to the Hebrews'), James, Jude and Revelation at the close of the New Testament, but there is no evidence that either he or the English Reformers shared Luther's doubts.

THE PESHITTA IN SYRIA

Sometime after AD 411, Bishop Rabbula of Edessa ordered a new translation of the Scriptures for the Syrian churches. Using the latest Greek manuscripts available, the Peshitta was widely used for a long time and fairly represented the canon used by the churches at Antioch and across Syria.[139] It did not contain 2 and 3 John, 2 Peter, Jude or the Apocalypse, but there were no 'rogue' entries either. From the numerous quotations in his extensive writings, it appears that John Chrysostom of Constantinople was using the same collection of books as the Peshitta. This is still the official canon of the Syrian Orthodox Church.[140]

CHURCH COUNCILS

The first ecumenical council at Nicaea, summoned by the Emperor Constantine in AD 335, apparently did not discuss a canon of books, even though the authority of the 'Scriptures' was often referred to. The issue at Nicaea was not the content of the canon, but the true deity of Christ. The Scriptures were the source of authority in the debate and the one thing that the delegates did not argue about was what constituted Scripture. That was fixed.

---

139 Westcott, *The Canon of the New Testament*, p. 292, comments on the translations into Syrian and Latin before the close of the second century: 'Combined with the original Greek they represent the New Testament Scriptures as they were read throughout the whole of Christendom towards the close of second century.'

140 Metzger, *The Canon of the New Testament*, p. 220. Parts of the churches in Syria to this day accept only twenty-two books. See F F Bruce, *The Canon of Scripture*, p. 215.

The first undisputed reference to the canon from a council of leaders comes in AD 397 at the third Council of Carthage. The list is precisely as we know it, and the Council made clear that it is 'what we have received from our fathers.' Heading the list is the injunction that: 'It was resolved that nothing should be read in church under the name of the divine scriptures except the canonical writings.' It was allowed, however, to read the stories of the martyrs on their anniversaries.

PERSECUTION

The increasing pressure upon the churches by government persecution also had an influence on the formation of the canon. According to Eusebius, on 23 February 303 under the Emperor Diocletian 'royal edicts were published everywhere, commanding that the churches be levelled to the ground and the Scriptures be destroyed by fire.'[141] It is unlikely that the Roman inquisitors could distinguish between Scriptures and other Christian literature—nor did they probably care—but it mattered to the Christians. It was a thorough search, as records of the time reveal, and at least three brave women were burned alive for refusing to hand over their sacred parchments. Few would pay the ultimate penalty unless they had good reason to believe that the 'parchments' were not less than the Scriptures.

Some devised a sneaky way out. Caecilian, the bishop of Carthage, hid his Scriptures and offered the writings of heretics instead. Those who handed over their scriptures were branded as *traditores* (those who surrender) by many. This led directly to a division among the churches. In AD 312 the church at Carthage rejected Caecilian for this act of treachery and elected Donatus instead, who promptly disciplined the *traditores*. The Donatists considered themselves the pure church and, in the time of Constantine, rejected any interference of the state in church affairs; the schism rumbled on for almost two hundred years.

Persecution had some effect, though not a decisive influence, on sharpening the line between canonical and other literature.

---

141 Eusebius, *Ecclesiastical History*, Book VIII, Ch. 2:4.

SUMMARY FROM AD 180

From AD 180 onwards, literally thousands of references and quotations were made in the writing of able leaders from almost all the New Testament books. Among all the church leaders, without any exception beyond the cults, the four Gospels, Acts and thirteen letters of Paul were accepted without question. No 'heretical' books seriously jockeyed for a place in the canon.

Before the close of the second century, both Tertullian and Clement of Alexandria were referring to the 'canonical' books as 'The New Testament'. The contents of the canon was by now assumed rather than debated. Only 2 Peter lacks a clear acceptance. Eusebius and Athanasius by the middle of the fourth century provide the clearest evidence of an agreed list of canonical books. That of Athanasius is identical to ours.

With the exceptions noted above, from the time of the apostles to Athanasius (AD 367), we have a united testimony for a consistent acceptance of New Testament books (and only those) from leaders as far apart as (in today's terms): Israel (Caesarea), Syria (Antioch), Turkey (Smyrna), Greece (Corinth), Italy (Rome), France (Lyons), Tunisia (Carthage), and Egypt (Alexandria).

Although no council of bishops had yet pronounced on the canon of the New Testament, by the time of Jerome and Augustine in the later fourth century it was considered to be fixed and agreed. Not until the Council at Carthage in AD 397 do we have an officially sanctioned list. Yet that list had been assumed by the majority of churches for more than one hundred years.

A summary of the earliest evidence of complete canons is not included in this book, but can be downloaded as a PDF. Go to https://www.dayone.co.uk/collections/books/all-you-need-to-know

6. Who wrote the books?

There can be little doubt about the identity of most of the writers of our New Testament books.

U ntil the nineteenth century, when the critical onslaught against the reliability of the Bible got underway, there was little doubt or debate over the authorship of most of the books of the New Testament. Those who still question the authorship of the books often betray what one critical scholar himself admits is 'a wilful blindness' to evade a solution 'they have already prejudged to be impossible.'[142]

Our evidence for who wrote the various books of the New Testament comes to us from three directions: First, many of the books, especially Paul's letters, include an introduction with the author's name; this has every right to be accepted as genuine unless or until it can be proven otherwise. Second, for other books, especially the four Gospels, there are early and long held traditions regarding the authorship; these also have a right to be taken seriously unless there is clear contrary evidence. Third, there are often internal evidences within the book itself to support the above two.

The four Gospels and Acts

We have seen in the previous two chapters that all the evidence is that only the four Gospels were used by the early church. Eusebius in the fourth century surveyed the evidence and concluded that the four Gospels 'are the only indisputable ones in the Church of God under heaven'.[143]

Later, false gospels were written mostly by the Gnostics (see chapter 8), but none of these ever competed for a place in the New Testament canon. As early as AD 150, Tatian for his *Diatessaron* used only our four in his

---

142 John A T Robinson, *Redating the New Testament* (SCM Press, London 1976), pp. 201–202.
143 Eusebius, *Ecclesiastical History*, Book 6, 25:4.

synopsis of the Gospels (see chapter 4), and similarly when Ammonius of Alexandria in AD 220 produced his *Harmonia*, listing the parallel passages of the Gospels, he also only used the four. Augustine in his fourth century *De Consensu Evangelistarum* discussed only the four Gospels and harmonised the parallel passages. The issue of what Gospels were being used by the churches for the authentic history of Jesus Christ was effectively closed almost as soon as they were written—before the end of the first century.

Today, there is a swing in favour of the evidence that the Gospels are not late writings but were penned early in the history of the Christian community; the idea that in the Gospels we cannot find the Jesus of history but only the whisper of the 'Christ of faith'—the faith of the third century church—is at last heading for its long-awaited grave. Even the *National Geographic* magazine, in publicising the translated *Gospel of Judas* (2005), accepted that the four Gospels were written between AD 65 to 95.[144] That was a significant claim since it places the four Gospels well before the close of the first century.

Whilst none of the Gospels carries a name for its authorship, the early and unquestioned acceptance of the traditional names bears significant weight. Since apostolic testimony was important for the early church, there would be no reason for Papias, writing shortly after the turn of the first century, to invent authors like Mark and Luke who were not actually apostles. If he was inventing names for an otherwise anonymous life of Christ, why did he not attribute them to one of the disciples of Christ?

THE GOSPEL OF MATTHEW

No name is attached to the opening text of this Gospel, although every available manuscript today includes the title 'according to Matthew'.

Papias (AD 125) wrote, 'Matthew composed the *logia* in the Hebrew tongue and everyone interpreted them as he was able…' In Romans 3:2 and Hebrews 5:12, the word *logia* refers to the Old Testament and

---

144 See the *National Geographic* time-line at nationalgeographic.com/lostgospel/timeline.html. Though their documentary on the National Geographic Channel claimed 'between 60 to 80 AD'.

Papias used the same word elsewhere to refer to the teaching of Jesus. Significantly he also used it to refer to Mark's Gospel. Since the word can simply mean 'writings', was Papias referring to some other, unknown, writings of Matthew? If so, this collection has vanished without trace, which is unlikely since such an important document of the sayings of Jesus would have been highly valued among the churches so early in the second century.

Irenaeus, only a few decades later than Papias, wrote, 'Matthew also issued a written gospel among the Hebrews in their own dialect, while Peter and Paul were preaching at Rome and laying the foundation of the church.'[145] If Irenaeus is quoting Papias, it is evident that he interpreted the logia as the Gospel of Matthew. If he is not quoting from Papias, then clearly Irenaeus independently believed Matthew wrote the Gospel.

Origen, one hundred years later, wrote similarly of Matthew's Gospel. Even if he also is copying from Papias, it shows the long-standing tradition from the turn of the first century. One scholar on this subject, comments, 'This evidence points to an unbroken tradition that Matthew wrote his Gospel in Hebrew, and advocates of any hypothesis which disagrees with this must suggest an adequate explanation of so consistent a tradition.'[146]

Because of the predictions of the destruction of the temple (Matthew 24) and Irenaeus' comment that it was written 'while Peter and Paul were preaching at Rome', it must have been written prior to AD 70 when Jerusalem was destroyed and by which time Peter and Paul had been martyred.

THE GOSPEL OF MARK

No other suggestion has ever been offered than the united testimony of Papias (AD 125), Irenaeus (AD 180), Clement of Alexandria (AD 200),

---

145 Irenaeus, *Against Heresies*, Book 3.1
146 Donald Guthrie, *New Testament Introduction*, Gospels and Acts (Tyndale Press, London 1966), p. 37. Guthrie's *New Testament Introduction* published in a single volume has established itself as the benchmark evangelical introduction to the New Testament. All critical views of authorship, date, destination, purpose etc are discussed in detail. This is the definitive resource for this subject and therefore will not be footnoted for each book.

Origen (AD 200) and Jerome (AD 400) that John Mark, the nephew of Barnabas and onetime travelling companion of the apostle Paul and Peter was the author of this Gospel under Peter's direction (Acts 15:39; Colossians 4:10; 2 Timothy 4:11; Philemon 24; 1 Peter 5:13).

According to the first church historian, Eusebius, writing early in the fourth century, it was Papias who confirmed the authorship of this Gospel:

'Mark having become the interpreter of Peter, wrote down accurately, though not in order, whatsoever he remembered of the things said or done by Christ. For he neither heard the Lord nor followed him, but afterward, as I said, he followed Peter, who adapted his teaching to the needs of his hearers, but with no intention of giving a connected account of the Lord's discourses, so that Mark committed no error while he thus wrote some things as he remembered them. For he was careful of one thing, not to omit any of the things which he had heard, and not to state any of them falsely.'[147]

There can be little doubt regarding the authorship of this Gospel; if it was not Mark, a more likely name of an apostle would have been added. The majority of biblical scholars accept that Mark must be dated at the very latest around AD 65 to 70, and some believe it was much earlier.

THE GOSPEL OF LUKE

The author of this Gospel does not give us his name, and since it was sent personally to Theophilus (Luke 1:3; Acts 1:1) there was evidently no need for him to. Although he does not specifically claim to be an eyewitness of the life of Christ, there is no conclusive reason to believe he was not. All he claims in his introduction is that he is aware of the records of those who were eyewitnesses 'from the first'. Luke promises that he has set out 'an orderly account' after careful and thorough research. His purpose is that Theophilus might 'know the certainty of the things you have been taught' (Luke 1:4).

The *Muratorian Canon*, Irenaeus, Clement of Alexandria, Tertullian (all before AD 220) and Origen (before AD 253) all claim that Luke was the author of both the Gospel and the Acts of the Apostles. If, as a few critics

---

147 Eusebius, *Ecclesiastical History*, Book 3, 39:15.

have suggested,[148] Luke was simply added to provide a named 'author', we would have expected the early church to add the name of an apostle, not the relatively insignificant colleague of Paul. Like Matthew and Mark, no other name for authorship has ever been attached to the Gospel of Luke.

THE ACTS OF THE APOSTLES

Both the Gospel of Luke and the Acts of the Apostles are addressed to the same man (Luke 1:3; Acts 1:1).[149] Acts refers to 'my former book' and there can hardly be any doubt that this is referring to the Gospel. Almost all scholars accept that the strong similarities in the two books of language and style leads to the obvious conclusion of a common author. The well-known 'we' passages (Acts 16:10–17, 20:5–15, 21:1–18, 27:1 to 28:16) identify the author as a travelling companion of Paul, and the references to his presence with Paul (Colossians 4:14; 2 Timothy 4:11; Philemon 24) confirm this. In the history of debate over the authorship of both this book and the Gospel, scholars from all persuasions have overwhelmingly accepted Luke as the author.[150]

For any portion of ancient literature, other than the New Testament, one piece of evidence would be almost conclusive in favour of an early date for at least the Gospel of Luke and the Acts. Robinson saw it, but he was not the first.[151] The book of Acts stops abruptly and leaves Paul under house arrest. There is no evidence of anything having been added or taken away from this ending. Only one reasonable explanation is possible, and that is that when Luke penned Acts, the rest of Paul's life had not been completed. Luke may have died before the outcome of Paul's trial, but clearly he had written his Gospel before Acts (Acts 1:1).[152]

---

148 H J Cadbury article 'The Tradition' in Foakes Jackson-Lake, *The Beginnings of Christianity*, vol. II, pp. 209–264.

149 In addition to Guthrie (above), see also F F Bruce, *The Acts of the Apostles* (Tyndale Press, London 1962 ed), pp. 1–10.

150 For details and a response to the dismissal by some critics of the relevance of the 'we' passages see Guthrie's *New Testament Introduction, Gospels and Acts*, pp. 94–98.

151 Robinson, *Redating the New Testament* as above.

152 The earliest tradition is that Luke died at the age of 84 in Greece where he wrote his Gospel. This is not impossible since he could have been around 60 when he travelled with Paul.

Anyone writing this story years later would most certainly have added an informative conclusion. Acts stops where it does because that is as far as the record of Paul's life had reached when Luke's account was sent to Theophilus.

THE GOSPEL OF JOHN

Because this Gospel is very different from the other three (which are known as the 'Synoptic Gospels')—it includes no parables for example—it is perhaps inevitable that its authorship has been debated in detail. The author nowhere gives us his name, but his attempts to conceal it often reveal it. He certainly claims to be an eyewitness: 'we have seen his glory' (John 1:14 and compare 1 John 1:1–4), and again in 19:35 and 21:24–25. The writer's evident knowledge of Jewish customs and history reveal him as a Jew, and his attention to detail reveals him as an eyewitness; see for example the exact number of fish caught and the precise distance of the boat from the land (21:8,11).

The references to 'the disciple whom Jesus loved' (13:23; 19:26; 20:2,8; 21:7,20) would be an unassuming way of leaving his name out of the account. Few seriously question that this can be anyone other than John. Alternative authors have been suggested in recent years, but none carries the strength of John's authorship.[153] Although nowhere in this Gospel is John mentioned by name, he is frequently mentioned in the Synoptics.

The differences between John's Gospel and the Synoptics, referred to above, is also an argument in favour of the apostle John being the author. Since it is generally agreed that this Gospel was compiled after the other three, it would need to be someone of clear apostolic authority who could introduce yet another account of the life of Jesus. The earliest witness to John as the author comes from the writing of Irenaeus (AD 180) who claimed that John was in Ephesus when he compiled it,[154] and he introduced John 20:31 with the claim 'As John, the disciples of the Lord

---

153 See Guthrie above, pp. 240–246.
154 Irenaeus, *Against Heresies*, Book 2:22.5. Eusebius claims that Irenaeus's authority for John's authorship was Polycarp.

verifies.'[155] All subsequent church leaders accepted without question that the author was John.

The 'Synoptic problem'

The 'Synoptic problem' is an attempt to discover which of the three 'Synoptic' Gospels came first, which relied on the others, and whether there was a common source for their material. This began as the 'fragmentary hypothesis' of Schliermacher in 1817, which has been largely abandoned today. The original debate assumed that none of the authors was an eyewitness and that the similarity in the Synoptic Gospels was evidence of common oral or written sources available to them.[156] Many critics accepted that the Gospels were written very late, at the earliest AD 70 to 100; this would rule out apostolic authorship.[157]

The differences in the detail of many narratives and the order of events, have been discussed at length by commentators. See Book 5 chapters 4 and 5 of this series. Various theories were suggested for the source material, including the possibility that for decades there was little more than a collection of isolated oral traditions. The exactness of common wording and common accounts, especially in Matthew and Luke, have led some to suggest a source called 'Q' as the written basis for the first three Gospels. A more obvious explanation is the fact that at least two of the three writers were eyewitnesses of the events they record.

The arguments for and against the hypothetical 'Q' are academic, inconclusive and confusing. Whether 'Q' was a single written source, a collection of several fragments, a combination of written and oral fragments, a purely oral tradition, whether it or they were used by Matthew, Mark and Luke—all, some or none—whether 'Q' included the nativity stories and the crucifixion stories, or whether 'Q' existed at

---

155 *Against Heresies*, Book 3.16:5.

156 A scholarly and straightforward introduction to this complex subject will be found in Guthrie, *New Testament Introduction*, pp. 114–211.

157 However, J A T Robinson (a liberal scholar) in *Redating the New Testament*, concluded all were written before AD 70. John Wenham, *Redating Matthew, Mark and Luke* (Hodder 1991) brings this to AD 50.

all, none of this we shall ever know—unless we find it or them. There is absolutely no record of a source 'Q'.

The New Testament letters

The letters in the New Testament were not written in the exact order that they appear in the earliest complete list of books, nor necessarily the order in which they appear in our Bible. (See chapters 4 and 5 here; and Book 6 chapter 6 of this series to see how they fit into the record of the Acts of the Apostles).

Since all the New Testament letters, except for Hebrews and the three from John, come with their names introducing them as part of the original text, the subject of authorship should be closed. The nineteenth century critics have been adequately answered. No other names were ever attached and therefore the responsibility is on those who deny the authorship to present conclusive alternative names. It is interesting to note that because the four Gospels and Acts have no author's name included in the text, critics dismissed the long-standing and well-documented traditional evidence for their authorship; however, since almost all the New Testament letters *do* have a name attached, it is dismissed as nearly irrelevant to the discussion of authorship. This commitment to a preconceived conclusion is evident.

The early Christian leaders, especially Irenaeus, Tertullian and Athanasius, were aware of attempts to present letters and gospels as if they came from an apostle (the *pseudepigrapha* that is introduced in chapter 8), yet they never questioned those in our New Testament.

The letters of Paul

The earliest orthodox canon of New Testament books (the *Muratorian Canon* c. AD 150) contains all thirteen of Paul's letters under his name. Subsequently Hebrews was occasionally added to this collection. However, exactly how and when Paul's letters were first gathered as a group is uncertain. All we can affirm is that before the middle of the second century Paul's thirteen letters were gathered into a collection under his name.

PAUL'S LETTER TO THE CHURCH AT ROME

No one seriously questions the ascription in 1:1 'Paul, a servant of Christ Jesus, called to be an apostle.' Paul sent this letter to the Christians at Rome during his three-month stay in Corinth in AD 57 (Acts 20:1–2). In the absence of any possibility for questioning the authorship of this book some have suggested that chapter 16 does not belong to it since Paul would not have sent so many greetings to a church he had never visited. This is purely hypothetical. Paul also sent a significant list of personal greetings to the church at Colossae, which he had never visited. These detailed greetings reveal how involved Paul was in the life of the churches, whether or not he had personally met them.

The fact that the beautiful doxology in 16:25–27 appears in some Greek manuscripts at the end of chapter 15 have led some to assume that the whole letter was originally a circular to the churches, or originally to Ephesus alone, to which the greetings in chapter 16 were added by Paul when it was sent to Rome. This is possible, but it is more likely that in some later copies of the letter the greetings were cut out as irrelevant for general use and the doxology was placed as the closure of chapter 15.

PAUL'S LETTERS TO THE CHURCH AT CORINTH

Paul's authorship is unquestioned. He wrote several letters to the church at Corinth, although only two have come down to us. In 1 Corinthians 5:9 he refers to a 'previous letter' in which he urged them not to associate with immoral people. This appears to have been misunderstood (1 Corinthians 5:10, 11) and, hearing of many disorders in the church at Corinth, Paul sent 1 Corinthians during his stay in Ephesus (AD 55–56). Having no news to encourage him, Paul paid a visit that he referred to as 'a painful visit' (2 Corinthians 2:1). On his return he wrote yet another letter 'out of great distress and anguish of heart and with many tears' (2 Corinthians 2:4). Meanwhile, he moved from Ephesus to Thessalonica in Macedonia where Titus arrived with some good news of the Corinthian repentance and Paul wrote what we know as his second letter to the Corinthians (AD 57). Shortly afterwards he spent three months in Corinth (Acts 20:2–3).

Inevitably, commentators and critics have disputed some of the above order of events, and some have even suggested that these two letters are simply compilations of a number of letters. However, the above outline is the most straightforward and fits perfectly with the known movements of Paul and the integrity of the themes with which Paul is dealing.

PAUL'S LETTER TO THE CHURCH OF GALATIA

The main point of discussion around this letter is not the authorship, which is rarely disputed, but its destination. The traditional view, until the nineteenth century, was that the letter was addressed to a number of churches in the northern part of the Roman province of Galatia; Paul presumably established many churches across this region in his second missionary journey (Acts 16:6). However, the renowned archaeologist and scholar, William Ramsay (see Book 5 chapter 2 in this series), suggested that the letter was more probably directed to churches in the region of South Galatia, a region known geographically as Phrygia.[158] This is now the commonly accepted view.

The significance of the destination is that if Paul was addressing the churches in the north, the letter must have been written sometime during his third missionary journey, as late as AD 56, whereas if it was written to the churches in the south it could have been written either shortly after or just before the Council of Jerusalem in Acts 15 as early as AD 48. This would be appropriate since the letter deals with the issue that was the 'hot topic' at that council namely, the influence of some of the Jewish converts perverting the true gospel of justification by faith alone.

PAUL'S LETTER TO THE EPHESIANS

Ephesians is one of a cluster of letters known as the 'captivity epistles': Ephesians, Colossians, Philippians and Philemon. The commonly accepted view that these were written when Paul was under house arrest in Rome (Acts 28), has been challenged by the suggestion that they were

---

158 William Mitchell Ramsay, *A Historical Commentary on St Paul's Epistle to the Galatians* (Hodder and Stoughton 1899).

written during Paul's captivity in Ephesus where he worked for three years (Acts 19; 20:31). Among a number of reasons for this is the fact that in 2 Corinthians 11:23 Paul declares that he has been in prison 'more frequently' (than the boasting self-appointed 'apostles'), yet up to this point the only recorded imprisonment is in Philippi (Acts 16). There is also an old tradition that Paul was in prison at Ephesus.

However, there are many events in Paul's more than twenty years of mission work that are not recorded in the Acts of the Apostles. We do not read of him being beaten five times or shipwrecked three times (2 Corinthians 11:24–25), so it is likely there were many unrecorded imprisonments. There is no mention of an imprisonment at Ephesus in Acts 19 where many of the incidents of his time there are detailed. Caesarea has also been suggested as a possible place for Paul's imprisonment, but few have supported this theory.

There should be no serious doubt as to the authorship of Ephesians. Not only does Paul introduce himself at the beginning, but he provides his name halfway (3:1), and much of the letter is in the first person and typically in Paul's style; his personal testimony in chapter 3 is evidently that of Paul himself. From the middle of the second century, this letter was widely distributed across the churches and always with Paul as the author; even the heretics were using it under Paul's authorship.

The arguments of extreme critics in the nineteenth century against Paul's authorship are based exclusively on linguistic and literary arguments which are always subjective and have little substance.[159] The suggestion that it was part of the anonymous *pseudepigrapha* of the first few centuries cannot be maintained because the churches were quick to recognise those false writings and, where known, would discipline the authors.

PAUL'S LETTER TO THE PHILIPPIANS

Clearly, Paul is a prisoner at the time of writing (1:7,13,16) and the possible place of imprisonment has been discussed above. Everything in this letter

---

159 Guthrie in *New Testament Introduction* has adequately presented and answered the critical views.

points to a Roman imprisonment. Since almost all scholars, of whatever persuasion, accept that this letter is genuinely from the apostle Paul, and there is no indication otherwise, we may safely leave the authorship there. The unbroken tradition and the internal evidence leave any unbiased commentator with no alternative.

Some scholars have suggested that 2:6–11 form a hymn that was composed separately from the rest of the epistle and added much later; however, this is a baseless hypothesis since there are no known manuscripts of this letter that do not include these verses. Whether Paul himself composed this 'hymn' or added one that was circulating among the Christians, it carries his authority and is a beautiful example of what the early churches may have been singing in their meetings.

PAUL'S LETTER TO THE COLOSSIANS AND TO PHILEMON
Only the most extreme critics dispute Paul's authorship of these two letters. They have never been separated (unfortunately they are separated in our Bibles), and Paul's name has always been attached to both. In his letter to the church at Colossae, Paul is clearly dealing with a grave issue of heresy facing the church, and the letter to Philemon is far too personal and pastoral to have any meaning unless it came from Paul.

PAUL'S LETTERS TO THE CHURCH AT THESSALONICA
Both letters were written whilst Paul was staying with Aquilla and Priscilla in Corinth around the year AD 51. Fortunately, Paul's authorship has been challenged by only the most radical critics and the earliest evidence always links Paul as the author. Besides the clear ascription at the beginning of each letter, the inclusion of details and names well known from the Acts of the Apostles, and the subject matter itself, all clearly point to Paul as the author.

PAUL'S LETTERS TO TIMOTHY AND TITUS
These are known as the 'Pastoral Epistles' because they are addressed to Timothy and Titus who were in the ministry at Ephesus and Crete respectively. It is generally accepted that they were written during Paul's

imprisonment at Rome (see for example 2 Timothy 1:16–18). Whether this was his first and only imprisonment in Rome or a second imprisonment just prior to his trial and execution under Nero is debated.

In spite of the fact that each of these letters opens with Paul as the author, that the internal details would either reveal the hand of a master forger or Paul himself, and that they have never circulated without the name of Paul, critics nevertheless have attacked this clear evidence. Once again, it was never questioned until the nineteenth century.

It is true that Marcion, the Gnostic heretic, did not include these in his canon of accepted books in the mid-second century; however, he similarly excluded Matthew, Mark and John, mutilated Luke and excluded all but ten of Paul's letters simply on the grounds that he rejected the entire Old Testament and anything that did not agree with his theology—Marcion is hardly an evidence to consider. Similarly, their absence from the *Chester Beatty Papyrus* P46 (see Book 4 chapter 3 in this series) is adequately explained by the fact that this incomplete manuscript of the third century contains only fifteen New Testament books. Apart from this, there is no external evidence to deny Paul's authorship. Arguments from the text itself in an attempt to prove that it had been written by a later admirer of Paul carry little weight.

The rest of the New Testament

THE LETTER TO THE HEBREWS

It is appropriate to begin with this letter since, whilst its authorship is widely debated, many do consider that it belongs to the apostle Paul. However, because no name is attached to it, no fewer than eight possibilities have been offered over the years of discussion: Paul, Barnabas, Luke, Clement, Sylvanus, Apollos, Philip, and Priscilla. This letter does not appear in the *Muratorian Canon* (which is incomplete anyway) or Marcion's Canon (unsurprisingly because of its frequent references to the Old Testament law).

The earliest evidence in favour of Paul's authorship comes from Clement of Alexandria (AD 153–216). Eusebius, a century after Clement, refers to Clement's own writing and affirms that Clement believed: 'The Epistle to the Hebrews is the work of Paul, and that it was written to the Hebrews in the Hebrew language; but that Luke translated it carefully and published it for the Greeks…' According to Eusebius, Clement believed that Paul withheld his name as a mark of humility, and not wishing to alienate the Hebrew Christians who were suspicious of him.[160]

Eusebius also referred to Origen of Alexandria (AD 180–253) who commented that the thoughts expressed are clearly those of Paul, and Origen concluded:

'Therefore, if any church holds that this epistle is by Paul, let it be commended for this. For not without reason have the ancients handed it down as Paul's. But who wrote the epistle, in truth, God knows.'

Origen added that some thought Clement of Rome wrote it and others that Luke was the author.[161] By the mid-third century the *Chester Beatty Papyrus* places it after Romans and the majority of Greek texts include it among Paul's letters.

However, the Western churches were more ambivalent. Tertullian, early in the third century, attributed it to Barnabas, and although Eusebius himself included it among Paul's letters he acknowledged that not all the churches believed it came from Paul and therefore some rejected it. Gradually the churches in the West accepted it as coming from Paul and this was not challenged until the time of the Reformation. Luther considered that Apollos wrote it. Calvin concluded it apostolic 'without hesitation', but was equally certain Paul was not the author. The debate continues. However, the earliest and most widely held tradition held Paul as the author.

THE LETTER FROM JAMES

Origen is the first Christian writer to refer to this epistle and he clearly accepted it as Scripture, although it was not accepted by the churches as quickly as the letters of Paul. Even by the time of Eusebius, early in the fourth century, he acknowledged it was disputed by some even though he

---

160 Eusebius, *Ecclesiastical History*, Book 6.14:2–4.
161 Eusebius, *Ecclesiastical History*, Book 6.25:11–14.

himself refers to it as genuine and written by James the Lord's brother. The fact that this letter is only occasionally quoted by the early church leaders cannot be taken as evidence against its acceptance. How many Christian preachers and authors today quote James compared with their use of Paul?

The author introduces himself as 'James, a servant of God and of the Lord Jesus Christ' (1:1), but James was a common first century name. If we assume the title is genuine—and there is no reliable reason to doubt it—there are only two James in the New Testament and one of those, the brother of John and son of Zebedee, was executed by Herod in AD 44 well before this letter was likely to have been written. That leaves us with James the brother of Jesus. Clearly the author must have been sufficiently well-known for him not to need to identify himself more specifically, and we may assume that his sincere humility prevented him from declaring himself as the Lord's brother.

There is no evidence of the book ever circulating without the name of James; although, with no evidence, some critics assume that the name was added later to give it authority. The argument against it coming from the brother of Jesus because the Greek is too good for a Galilean peasant, is also used against 1 and 2 Peter and is answered below.

If the author is the brother of our Lord, it will have been written before AD 62 because, according to the Jewish historian Josephus, James was stoned to death in Jerusalem on the orders of Ananus, the High Priest of that year.[162] A date somewhere before AD 48 is likely, since James deals with the importance of good works without guarding himself against the issues confronting the council in Jerusalem which was held in that year.

THE LETTERS OF PETER

1 PETER

There had been no doubt regarding the genuineness of the title in 1:1 that Peter was the writer of this letter until the nineteenth century. Scholars, determined to deny the unanimous agreement of all the early church

---

162 Josephus, *Antiquities*, XX.9 1.

leaders, denied Peter's involvement chiefly because of the excellent Greek style, the wide vocabulary and the knowledge of the Greek Old Testament (the *Septuagint*) that the letter reveals. Unlike Paul, nowhere do we read of Peter, an Aramaic speaking Jewish fisherman, receiving an education that would equip him for such a literary achievement.

In response to this, we should note that the word in Acts 4:13 does not mean 'ignorant' but 'unschooled', without a formal education. More than thirty years separated the time when Peter was called from his fishing industry to writing this letter, and that is more than adequate time for his self-taught education to equip him for writing excellent Greek. Critics appear to have forgotten that John Bunyan, acknowledged as a giant of seventeenth century literature, was an 'unschooled' pot-mender by trade; a century later William Carey who, among many academic attainments, became professor of languages at Fort William College in India, was a cobbler before he left for India; John Newton, with only two years of inferior education, taught himself to read his Bible in Hebrew and Greek and corresponded with Dutch theologians in Latin; and Benjamin Franklin, the American author, politician, diplomat, publisher, scientist and inventor, similarly had no more than two years of formal education. Those examples alone should be sufficient to silence for ever the argument against Peter on the ground of language and style.

Other objections include the facts that the writer is clearly addressing a people suffering persecution at a time when widespread persecution of Christians had not yet begun, and Peter does not appear to have had much association with the churches across Asia that he addresses (1:1). This latter point is answered by the fact that Peter disappears from the history of the Acts of the Apostles in chapter 15 and no one can be sure of his movements after that; who knows where he may have travelled?

As for the argument about persecution, Paul is equally clear that persecution is both present and inevitable: 'In fact, everyone who wants to live a godly life in Christ Jesus will be persecuted' (2 Timothy 3:12). The 'fiery trial' (a literal translation of 1 Peter 4:12) may well refer to the cruelties of Nero which we know from secular historians included the burning of Christians.

Since no manuscripts of 1 Peter appear without his name at the front, and since all the early church leaders accepted Peter's authorship without question, and since someone must have written it, the theories to deny Peter as author, with no alternative name to offer, should not significantly concern us.

2 PETER

No manuscript of 2 Peter lacks his name at the opening, and the author lays claim to being an eyewitness of the life of Christ, and a colleague of Paul. However, unlike almost all the New Testament books, few of the early church leaders refer to it. Origen of Alexandria (AD 240) is almost our only definite source. He used it six times and clearly accepted that it was from the hand of Peter; he referred to Peter 'sounding aloud with the two trumpets of his letters'.[163] Origen indicated that some had doubts about its apostolic authorship, but he himself did not. Its absence from the *Muratorian Canon* is not greatly significant since that document is incomplete and it also omits 1 Peter which was never in doubt in AD 150. By the early fourth century, Eusebius commented that most churches accepted it even though he himself had doubts. 2 Peter was never rejected by the churches even though some took longer to accept it, perhaps because a copy had not reached them.

The common argument against Peter's authorship is that the Greek is so different from 1 Peter. In 1907 J B Mayor, calculated that there were 100 words common to the two books and 600 different words.[164] However, in 1965 A Q Morton ran the two books through a computer and concluded that they were 'linguistically indistinguishable' (in other words, from the same author). Some liberal scholars simply responded that this only proved that using computers was a waste of time![165] Long ago, when responding to similar critical arguments to show different authorship

---

163 Origen, *Homilies in Joshua* vii.1.

164 J B Mayor, *The Epistle of St Jude and Second Epistle of St Peter*, 1907. Quoted in Donald Guthrie, *New Testament Introduction*, Vol. 3, p.162.

165 A Q Morton 'Statistical Analysis and New Testament Problems' in *The Authorship and Integrity of the New Testament* (SPCR Theological Collection 1965). Quoted in Robinson, *Redating the New Testament*, p.185.

within Old Testament books, Robert Dick Wilson pointed out that Milton used hundreds of words and phrases in some of his works that he did not use in any other—yet no one suggests a different authorship.[166]

Careful scholarship has noted the significant similarity of the two letters in their use of Psalms, Proverbs and Isaiah, the reference to Noah (1 Peter 3:19–22: 2 Peter 2:5; 3:5–6) and the high view of the prophetic Scriptures (1 Peter 1:10–12 and 2 Peter 1:20–21). There is no convincing reason why the letter did not come from the apostle Peter.

THE LETTER OF JUDE

The opening sentence should settle the question of authorship. Although Jude was a common name, the writer identifies himself as 'a brother of James'. Since, as we have seen above, the apostle James was executed by Herod in AD 44 (Acts 12:2), it is evident that we are intended to think of the James who was a brother of Jesus, a leader in the church at Jerusalem (Acts 15:13; Mark 6:3), and the author of the letter under his name.

Jude's letter was widely known across the early churches—certainly by the *Muratorian Canon* and in Alexandria by Tertullian, Clement, Origen, and Didymus, and in Caesarea by Eusebius. No one questioned the authorship, which is evidence that the author had some connection with an apostle as well as with the Lord himself. A few alternative names have been suggested, but with no evidence.

The close parallels, especially between Jude and 2 Peter 2, have been well noted by commentators; the description of false teachers is almost identical. The question is, who copied who? This need not affect the question of authorship.[167] Since Peter and Jude knew each other, there is no reason why their letters may not contain common subject matter about which they had either discussed or corresponded.

---

166 Robert Dick Wilson, *A Scientific Investigation of the Old Testament* (Marshall Brothers Ltd, London and Edinburgh 1926), p.162. Wilson had studied the Qu'ran in the Arabic and asked why the 32 words expressing the same idea there are not also considered evidence of different authorship?
167 Guthrie provides an excellent summary of the arguments on both sides in *New Testament Introduction*, pp.240–247.

THE THREE LETTERS OF JOHN

The first letter, and the letter to the Hebrews, are the only two New Testament letters that do not designate the author. However, the claim to have been an eyewitness throughout the life of Christ is significant (1:1–3). Either this is the record of an eyewitness, or else the writer of this beautiful letter, containing such a high standard of morality and Christian holiness, is a supreme liar. The similarity of its teaching with that of the Gospel of John, and its apostolic authority (4:6) is accepted by all but the most extreme critics. The authorship of both the Gospel and this letter stand together.

Irenaeus (AD 180) was in no doubt that John was the author. He introduced 1 John 2:18 with 'John testified to us in his Epistle', and similarly attributed 1 John 4:1 and 5:1 to the same author.[168] Polycarp, who was martyred in AD 155, quoted 1 John 4:3 as apostolic authority, although he does not refer to the author by name.[169]

The author of the second and third letters introduces himself as 'The elder'. Some who are determined to deny the apostolic authorship suggest that 'the elder' of the next two letters is the same as the author of 1 John— an unknown and unexplained anonymous author who may also have used the name John. However, Irenaeus is equally clear that the second letter is by John the apostle when he quotes 2 John 1:7.[170] He makes no mention of a separate 'John the Elder'.

In the early centuries, there are few quotations or allusions to the two short letters, which is not surprising for two very personal letters that may not have appeared of great relevance for the churches generally. One scholar (C H Dodd) has suggested that the subjects of 2 and 3 John are so relatively unimportant that it is hard to understand why anyone should bother to invent them. Clement, Origen and Dionysius, all from Alexandria, were aware of these letters but without committing themselves to an author.

---

168 Irenaeus, *Against Heresies*, Book 3.16:5,8.
169 Polycarp, *To the Philippians* vii.
170 Irenaeus, *Against Heresies*, Book 3.16:8.

All commentators agree that there are close similarities of theme and expression between all three of these letters. Some phrases are identical and many more are similar. Compare for example 1 John 2:23, 3:6 and 4:20 with 2 John 9 and 3 John 11. This strongly suggests the same hand in each. There are no convincing reasons to doubt John's authorship of all three letters attributed to him.

THE REVELATION OF JOHN (THE APOCALYPSE)

The early church leaders had little doubt that the apostle John was the author of this book. Well before the close of the second century it was known by the *Shepherd of Hermas*, the *Muratorian Canon*, Justin, Melito, Theophilus of Antioch, Irenaeus, Tertullian, Hippolytus, Clement and Origen of Alexandria and others. In each case the apostle John was known to be the writer of the Apocalypse. Apart from Marcion and a few other heretics, the Western churches almost unanimously accepted John's authorship. In the East, Dionysius disputed the authorship but not its right to be in the canon of Scripture; he suggested either John Mark or an unknown John of Ephesus.

Most of the arguments against authorship by the apostle John are based around the style of writing and the differences in Greek from the Gospel. These arguments are always subjective and do not sufficiently consider the completely different genre in the apocalyptic language of this book and the fact that much was given in the form of revelation.

What is certain, is that no one should dispute that the author is John (1:1,4,9;22:8), that the only John who historically easily fits into the role is the apostle, and that the earliest church leaders, with Dionysius the single exception, considered John the apostle to be author.

7. Helpful letters not in the Bible

In the first two hundred years after the apostles, there was helpful Christian writing that, although often popular, was not placed in the canon of New Testament books.

The false gospels and epistles that circulated during the two hundred years following the death and resurrection of Jesus Christ, were an undoubted threat to the Christian Church. This, together with increasing persecution from the authorities, forced many able leaders to defend the truth. Their letters, though mostly full of valuable instruction, might well have found their way into the canon of the New Testament—but not one of them did. Nor did their authors intend them to, and they were often quick to distance their own authority from that of the apostles. The second century was a busy time for writing, and this sample fairly represents the whole. It will also introduce some of the significant leaders of that time.

Books for the Christians

DIDACHE

Discovered in 1875, the *Didache*, or the 'Teaching' of the twelve apostles, is possibly the earliest non-canonical Christian document on record. It is thought to have been written somewhere between AD 50 and 80 (though a few scholars place it as late as the fourth century), and its content is generally in line with the New Testament teaching. Two clear quotations come from Matthew's Gospel, and other New Testament books are alluded to. *Didache* is not a book of theology but of practice, and as such was useful for the churches, although it adds nothing of any significance to the canonical books. The author is unknown and it was never accepted into the canon of the church. Athanasius thought it might be canonical, and Eusebius was equally certain that it was not.

The *Didache* deals with the Way of Life and the Way of Death (chapters 1–6); baptism, fasting, and Communion (chapters 7–10); caring for travelling prophets and teachers (chapters 11–15); and finally a brief warning about the coming anti-Christ before the return of the Saviour (chapter 16).

Here are just two excerpts:

'Thou shalt do no murder, thou shalt not commit adultery, thou shalt not corrupt boys, thou shalt not commit fornication, thou shalt not steal, thou shalt not deal in magic, thou shalt do no sorcery, thou shalt not murder a child by abortion nor kill them when born, thou shalt not covet thy neighbour's goods, thou shalt not perjure thyself, thou shalt not bear false witness, thou shalt not speak evil, thou shalt not cherish a grudge, thou shalt not be double-minded nor double-tongued.'[171]

On the subject of baptism, clearly adult baptism is the only mode that is recognised:

'But concerning baptism, thus shall ye baptize. Having first recited all these things, baptize in the name of the Father and of the Son and of the Holy Spirit in living [running] water. But if thou hast not living water, then baptize in other water; and if thou art not able in cold, then in warm. But if thou hast neither, then pour water on the head thrice in the name of the Father and of the Son and of the Holy Spirit. But before the baptism let him that baptizes and him that is baptized fast, and any others also who are able; and thou shalt order him that is baptized to fast a day or two before.'[172]

EPISTLE OF BARNABAS

For some, this epistle stood on what Bruce Metzger calls 'the fringe of the canon'[173] and it was included at the end of *Codex Sinaiticus* in the mid-fourth century; one of our earliest complete Greek texts of the New Testament. See in this series Book 4 chapter 3. However, by this time Eusebius had no hesitation in listing both *Hermas* and *Barnabas* among the books 'rejected' as having no part in the canon.

---

171 The *Didache*, 2:2.
172 The *Didache*, 7:1–7.
173 Bruce Metzger, *The Canon of the New Testament* (Oxford University Press, Oxford 1987), p.188.

Its authorship, date and destination are unknown. There is no evidence in favour of the author being Barnabas, the companion of Paul.[174] Clement of Alexandria was the first to ascribe it to that Barnabas, but Clement died around AD 216. It is thought to have been composed late in the first or early in the second century.

Apparently, the old problem of the Judaisers that Paul had had to deal with had not gone away, and some were still insisting that Gentile converts should adopt many of the Jewish ceremonies. Barnabas, whoever he was, would have none of it, and in his attempt to dismiss the relevance of the Old Testament ceremonies, he indulged in some highly fanciful argument,[175] and even suggested that the building of the temple was a mistaken understanding of what God really meant. There is some sound biblical reasoning as well. It closes with an exposition of the commandments and a warning against the deeds of 'The Black One'.

Even a quick read shows why the book had only transient attraction among the churches. Its method is extravagant and at times trivial and foolish. Its chief appeal was excessive spiritualising that was, unfortunately, popular among many in the early centuries of the church.

SHEPHERD OF HERMAS

Undoubtedly the *Shepherd of Hermas* was the most popular non-canonical book read among the early churches. There is some evidence for the author writing late in the first century but better evidence for a date around the mid-second century since the *Muratorian Canon* claims that it was written 'very recently, in our times, in the city of Rome' in the days when Pius (who died around AD 154) was bishop of Rome. It makes no claim to be apostolic, or even to have been written in association with an apostle.

As late as the fourth century *Hermas* was still used as an instruction manual for young converts and, together with the *Epistle of Barnabas*, it is attached at the end of the fourth century *Codex Sinaiticus*. By the close

---

174 Kirsopp Lake, *The Apostolic Fathers* (published London 1912), vol. I, pp. 337–339.
175 The *Epistle of Barnabas*, Ch. 9.

of the fourth century, Jerome claimed that although it was still used in Greece, it was virtually unknown among the Western churches.[176]

Hermas is a slave in Rome who receives visions of the church in the guise of an old woman. The third vision is of a white tower, also representing the church, and it forms a parable of various types of people associated with the church, including leaders, the faithful, reprobates, worldly and so on. There is a strong warning against riches: 'When you were rich you were useless.'[177] Seven women supporting the tower are: Faith, Self-restraint, Simplicity, Guilessness, Chastity, Intelligence and Love. In the fifth vision, we are introduced to the Shepherd who has been 'sent by a most venerable angel to dwell with you the remaining days of your life.' The Shepherd gives Hermas twelve commandments that exhort to Christian living; then follows ten 'Similitudes' [allegories] that come to Hermas from the Shepherd at various times.

The author possessed a vivid imagination and he records his visions in great detail. It is a long read of over thirty-seven thousand words, and is certainly tedious. The author is undoubtedly sincere and pious and it is basically a book of good morality and stern self-discipline. Sadly, there is little of the work of Christ or the gospel, and the Shepherd is stronger on morality than he is on theology. Perhaps the best way to describe Hermas is a mixture of the parables of the Old Testament prophets, the Apocalypse of John the Apostle, and the literature of John Bunyan—without the authority of the first two or the clarity of all three.

The *Muratorian Canon* is clear that though it may be read privately it should not be read in the churches since it is 'after the time' of the apostles.[178] Later in the second century, Tertullian was adamant that this book did not belong in the canon; it was, 'habitually judged by every council of Churches [even among the heretics] among apocryphal and false [writings].'[179] Origen suggested that the author may be the

---

176 Metzger, p. 236 from *De Perpetua Virginitate*, III.10.
177 The *Shepherd of Hermas*, Vision 3, Ch. 6.
178 The *Muratorian Canon*, 75–81 in Bruce Metzger, *The Canon of the New Testament*, Appendix IV, p. 307.
179 Tertullian, *On Modesty*, Ch. 10.

Hermas referred to in Romans 16:14 and even that it might be 'divinely inspired' [180]—but he was alone on both suggestions.

Wise words from wise leaders

In addition to these anonymous documents, there were many helpful letters written by the church leaders before the close of second century. They did not hide their authorship and made no claim to apostolic authority; there was never any question of them being confused with the canonical Scriptures.

CLEMENT OF ROME

The church at Corinth was in a mess—yet again! Paul had taken two or three letters to sort them out, but that was four decades ago. It was left to Clement to send them a stiff correction because their bad behaviour, according to Clement, was worse than before.

Clement is thought to have been the third leader (bishop) at Rome, but we know virtually nothing about Linus and Anacletus who preceded him, except that Irenaeus mentions them and that Linus is the one referred to by Paul in 2 Timothy 4:21.[181] Because of the early date of the letter, somewhere around AD 96, it is generally considered that the author may be the Clement referred to in Philippians 4:3 as a 'fellow-worker' with Paul. There are many references in his letter that imply a close association with Paul, and Irenaeus claims that Clement knew Paul so well and had listened to him so often that he 'might be said to have the preaching of the Apostles still echoing [in his ears].' [182] It is not known for certain how Clement met his death, but one story is that he was tied to an anchor and thrown into the sea.

Clement began his lengthy letter by apologising for not having written sooner—a common opener for correspondents in all ages—and set himself to attend to the issue on which they had sought his counsel, namely: 'The shameful and detestable sedition, utterly abhorrent to the

---

180 Origen, *Commentary on Romans*, 10:31.
181 Irenaeus, *Against Heretics*, Book III, Ch. 3:3.
182 As above.

elect of God, which a few rash and self-confident persons have kindled to such a pitch of frenzy.'[183]

Although Clement could commend them for many good things at Corinth, their peace and humility and their reputation among the churches had been shattered by division. Clement traced examples of division in the Old Testament and reminded the Corinthians of the sufferings and martyrdom of Peter and Paul, and others more recently. He then turned his readers to Christ: 'Let us look steadfastly to the blood of Christ, and see how precious that blood is to God, which, having been shed for our salvation, has set the grace of repentance before the whole world.'[184] He promised them full forgiveness if they follow this path.

The letter is thoroughly grounded in Old Testament Scripture with many examples and quotations; here and there the Gospels are used as well. Clement pleaded, 'Let us cleave, therefore, to those who cultivate peace with godliness, and not to those who hypocritically profess to desire it.'[185] Christ is put forward as an example of humility, and this is followed by the prophets who 'went about proclaiming the coming of Christ.'

Then the pastor addressed the various sections of the church:

'Let us reverence the Lord Jesus Christ, whose blood was given for us; let us esteem those who have the rule over us; let us honour the aged among us; let us train up the young men in the fear of God; let us direct our wives to that which is good. Let them exhibit the lovely habit of purity [in all their conduct]; let them show forth the sincere disposition of meekness ... Let your children be partakers of true Christian training; let them learn of how great avail humility is...'[186]

Clement continued by reminding them of the promise of resurrection and the gospel of salvation by faith and not by works,[187] and finally, just as in the army not all are in command, and in the body all parts work

---

183 *Clement's letter to the Corinthians*, Ch.1.
184 As above, Ch. 7.
185 As above, Ch.15.
186 As above, Ch. 21.
187 As above, Ch. 35.

harmoniously together, so it should be in the church.[188] Clement set out his order for the church: Christ was sent by the Father and in turn he sent out his apostles: 'Both these appointments, then, were made in an orderly way, according to the will of God.' Clement is certain that those:

'Who have blamelessly served the flock of Christ in a humble, peaceable, and disinterested spirit, and have for a long time possessed the good opinion of all, cannot be justly dismissed from the ministry. For our sin will not be small, if we eject from the episcopate those who have blamelessly and holily fulfilled its duties ... We see that you have removed some men of excellent behaviour from the ministry, which they fulfilled blamelessly and with honour.'[189]

The behaviour of such people is 'disgraceful' and 'unworthy' of their Christian profession. Clement's final appeal must be in his own words:

'You therefore, who laid the foundation of this sedition, submit yourselves to the presbyters, and receive correction so as to repent, bending the knees of your hearts. Learn to be subject, laying aside the proud and arrogant self-confidence of your tongue. For it is better for you that you should occupy a humble but honourable place in the flock of Christ, than that, being highly exalted, you should be cast out from the hope of His people.'[190]

This powerful pastoral letter, so full of wisdom and Scripture, was still being read at Corinth decades after the church first received it.[191] It is therefore significant that the letter of Clement was never a contender for inclusion in the canon.

IGNATIUS OF ANTIOCH
Ignatius was making his slow journey from Antioch to Rome under guard, knowing that at the end he would be thrown to the wild beasts for the

---

188 As above, Ch. 37.
189 As above, Ch. 44.
190 As above, Ch. 57.
191 According to Eusebius in his *Ecclesiastical History*, Book iii, Ch. 16. He describes it as 'of considerable length and of remarkable merit'. Dionysius of Corinth, around AD 165, refers to the fact that the letter from Clement was still read for valuable 'admonition', *Ecclesiastical History*, Book IV, Ch. 23:11.

sport of a roaring crowd. On his way, sometime in the year AD 115, and expecting inevitable martyrdom of the cruellest kind, Ignatius, known also as Theophorus, wrote six pastoral letters to churches, and one to his friend Polycarp. Those seven are the final testament of a condemned man. His letter to the Christians at Rome must have come as a painful prelude of what lay ahead:

'Let me be given to the wild beasts, for through them I can attain unto God. I am God's wheat, and I am ground by the teeth of wild beasts that I may be found pure bread [of Christ]. Rather entice the wild beasts, that they may become my sepulchre and may leave no part of my body behind, so that I may not, when I am fallen asleep, be burdensome to any one … Come fire and cross and grappling with wild beasts, wrenching of bones, hacking of limbs, crushing of my whole body, come cruel tortures of the devil to assail me. Only be it mine to attain unto Jesus Christ.' [192]

This cluster of letters—that Polycarp later gathered and treasured and that the church at Philippi was so eager to obtain copies of—are full of pastoral care and good instruction, not least his warm and gentle letter to Polycarp. It is significant that this number of seven letters is greatly exceeded by the eleven that are listed as 'other spurious epistles in the name of Ignatius'—not only the apostolic books suffered from forgeries.

Ignatius was the bishop of the church at Smyrna, and in all his letters his theme is much the same: an encouragement to remain united under their bishop, and a warning of the many false teachers that were invading the churches and enticing people away. Writing to the Ephesians, Ignatius was anxious that he should not be judged as pretending to any superior authority: 'I do not issue orders to you, as if I were some great person.' [193] He warns them against 'Some most worthless persons [who] are in the habit of carrying about the name of Jesus Christ in wicked guile, while yet they practise things unworthy of God, and hold opinions contrary to the doctrine of Christ.' [194]

---

192 Ignatius, *The Epistle to the Romans*, I4:2–5, 5:14–15.
193 As above, Ch. 3.
194 As above, Ch. 7.

With a clear stab at the growing influence of the Gnostics, he warned the Philadelphians, 'If any one confesses Christ Jesus the Lord, but denies the God of the law and of the prophets, saying that the Father of Christ is not the Maker of heaven and earth, he has not continued in the truth any more than his father the devil, and is a disciple of Simon Magus, not of the Holy Spirit.'[195]

To his own people at Smyrna, Ignatius wrote from Troas. His gratitude for their prayers, love and provision of his needs, together with the fact that they were not ashamed of his bonds, is a moving example of the relationship of a first century pastor with his people.

These letters are not theological treatise but pastoral appeals; they breathe the atmosphere of a Christian leader who is living close to God and whose spirit would encourage the churches to peace, harmony and truth. The letters of Ignatius were never considered for inclusion in the canonical list.

POLYCARP OF SMYRNA

It was Sunday 23 February AD 155 when the soldiers burst into the farmstead where Polycarp the leader at Smyrna had taken refuge. The old man of eighty-six years ordered a meal to be laid for them and invited the solders to eat and drink as much as they desired, while he spent just one hour in prayer before they took him away. Arriving at the stadium in Rome, the proconsul, Statius Quadratus, urged him to have consideration to his age and to worship the emperor. This, according to *The Martyrdom of Polycarp*, was his reply: 'Fourscore and six years have I been his servant, and he has done me no wrong. How then can I blaspheme my King who saved me?'[196]

When threatened with wild beasts, the old warrior replied 'Call for them.' The proconsul warned of being burned with fire, and he was treated with the response: 'You threaten that fire which burns for a season and after a little while is quenched, for you are ignorant of the fire of the future judgment

---

195 *Ignatius to the Philadelphians*, Ch. 6.
196 *The Martyrdom of Polycarp*, 9:12.

and eternal punishment, which is reserved for the ungodly.' As the soldiers were about to nail him to the stake, Polycarp requested, 'Leave me as I am; for he who has granted me to endure the fire will grant me also to remain at the pile unmoved, even without the security which you seek from the nails.'

So, Polycarp died and his story was told and retold among the churches.

Polycarp had been a disciple of the apostle John, and apparently he wrote a number of letters, although only his letter to the church at Philippi has survived. The church had evidently requested copies of the letters that Polycarp received from Ignatius who, on his own journey to martyrdom, was given hospitality at Smyrna by Polycarp. Polycarp was only too happy to respond to the request of the Philippians and sent copies by the hand of Crescens.

The letter contains no theology and adds nothing to the canonical books. However, it is full of sound ethical instructions for the safety of the church. He encouraged the Christians at Philippi to stand firm in the faith, avoid heresy and to maintain a life of good works. He would also like to receive any news of the welfare of Ignatius—if he had not already died.

Polycarp is careful to distance his own leadership and authority from that of the apostle Paul; there was to be no danger of the Philippians equating Polycarp, or anyone else of his day, with apostolic authority:

'Neither am I, nor is any other like unto me, able to follow the wisdom of the blessed and glorious Paul, who when he came among you taught face to face with the men of that day the word which concerns truth carefully and surely; who also, when he was absent, wrote a letter to you, into the which if you look diligently, you shall be able to be built up unto the faith given to you.' [197]

Undoubtedly, the letter that Paul had written to the church at Philippi more than a century earlier, was still a prized possession among them.

PAPIAS OF HIERAPOLIS

Papias is a mysterious figure of whom we know very little except that he was leader in the church at Hierapolis in Phrygia, where Paul's fellow-

---

197 *The Epistle of Polycarp to the Philippians*, 3:2–3.

worker Epaphras had worked hard (Colossians 4:12–13). According to Irenaeus, who was writing in AD 180, Papias lived 'long ago' and he was a friend of Polycarp; this means that he must have been alive at the turn of the first century. Only small fragments of the work of Papias have survived, which is frustrating since he wrote a lengthy *Expositions of the Oracles of the Lord*. He gathered most of his 'sayings' from word of mouth, but insisted that they had to be from the apostles.

JUSTIN MARTYR OF ROME

In Justin, we have a very different kind of writing. These are not pastoral letters but a vigorous, even aggressive, defence of the Christian faith from a great mind steeped in the ability to argue a case well and forcefully.

Justin was a Gentile born in Samaria around the year AD 114. He was a philosopher by interest, education and practice, but it was the emptiness of philosophy—and he had tried most of them—and observing the courage of Christians under torture and death, that led him to Christ.[198] He was well-travelled and spent time in Ephesus and Rome. It was in Rome that the philosophers plotted against him and he was martyred, probably when Marcus Aurelius was emperor.

Some of the most important writing of the second century comes from his pen. He wrote a lengthy work in defence of the Christian faith, addressed to the Emperor and the Senate, and a shorter protest against the treatment of Christians by Prefect Urbinus, and also an even more lengthy letter to Trypho the Jew, demonstrating that Jesus was the Messiah. These three are clearly his own work, although there are many other writings that are still disputed as to whether they belong to him or not.

The first appeal of Justin was addressed to the emperor Antoninus Pius (AD 138–161), and through him to the whole Senate and the people. It was written between AD 153 and 155. Justin asked for justice and truth. It is surely unfair that Christians should be punished simply because they bear that name, without any investigation. Let their lives be judged. They are charged with atheism for abandoning the national gods: 'And we confess

---

198 His own story is largely told in his *second Apology*, Chs 3 and 12.

that we are atheists, so far as gods of this sort are concerned, but not with respect to the most true God ... we are not atheists, worshipping as we do the Maker of this universe.'[199] Justin quoted freely from the philosophers Plato, Socrates and others, and then, dangerously, showed the folly of worshipping idols which are 'soulless and dead'.

Justin defended the morality of Christians by quoting extensively from the words of Christ found in the Gospels, and included the Lord's encouragement to civil obedience. Then he turned his fire towards the immorality of paganism, including the cruel practice of leaving unwanted children to die on the mountains:

'We have been taught that to expose newly-born children is the part of wicked men; and this we have been taught lest we should do any one an injury, and lest we should sin against God ... there are some who prostitute even their own children and wives, and some are openly mutilated for the purpose of sodomy; and they refer these mysteries to the mother of the gods.'[200]

All this is contrasted to the chastity of the Christians.

Perhaps Justin thought he had gone far enough in his strident criticism of paganism, so he changed tack. It was now time to preach the gospel. He began with the Old Testament prophecies of Jesus—an issue he would deal with in great detail in his debate with Trypho the Jew—and showed the birth, life, death, resurrection and ascension of the Messiah all in fulfilment of Old Testament prophecy. When he came to the cross, Justin explained well the purpose of Christ's death, but allowed himself a flight of fancy when he insisted that the symbol of the cross is all around us, from the sails of the ship, to the form of the plough and implements, to the human body erect and with outstretched arms. Justin's parting shot in his first *Apology* was to warn the Emperor and the Senate: 'For we forewarn you, that you shall not escape the coming judgment of God, if you continue in your injustice.'

The second *Apology* is directed against the injustice of Prefect Urbinus; it is much shorter but no less potent: 'If he assails us without having read

---

199 Justin Martyr, first *Apology*, Chs 6 and 42.
200 Justin Martyr, first *Apology*, Ch. 27.

the teachings of Christ, he is thoroughly depraved, and far worse than the illiterate, who often refrain from discussing or bearing false witness about matters they do not understand.'[201]

Justin then challenged the supposed thinkers, and demonstrated that both the Greek and Roman philosophers and poets were close to the truth when they mocked the gods and revealed the foolishness of pagan worship.

Finally, he appealed that his *Apology* should be published for all to read: 'And we therefore pray you to publish this little book, appending what you think right, that our opinions may be known to others, and that these persons may have a fair chance of being freed from erroneous notions and ignorance of good … And would that you also, in a manner becoming piety and philosophy, would for your own sakes judge justly.'[202]

Whether or not the emperor read this defence of the Christian faith is doubtful, but even if Titus Aelius Adrianus Antoninus Pius Augustus Caesar (as Justin styled him) took time out for a long read, it did Justin little good: around AD 165 he was condemned to death by the prefect Rusticus, and with six companions was tortured and beheaded.

Justin's theology is sound and his work is full of Christ. He showed himself to be a master at apologetics, even claiming that Plato gained his understanding of creation from the words of Moses.[203] His work must have been a source of encouragement and ammunition for the Christians in their battle against Romans, heretics and Jews alike. But it was never a contender for inclusion in the canon of the New Testament.

CLEMENT OF ALEXANDRIA

Born in AD 153 Clement was a pagan philosopher, like Justin, but when he became a Christian he took on the mantle of one of the church's greatest teachers and apologists of the second century. A leader in the teaching school at Alexandria he turned that city into 'the brain of Christendom' until in 202 the persecutions under Septimus Severus forced him to flee.

---

201 Justin Martyr, second *Apology*, Ch. 3.
202 As above, Chs 14–15.
203 Justin Martyr, first *Apology*, Ch. 59.

Somehow Clement survived the cruel years of the emperors Severus and Caracalla and he died at almost seventy years of age.

Clement is known especially for three works: the *Exhortation to the Heathen*, the *Instructor*, and the *Miscellanies*. His writing reveals his immense learning and at least one scholar has recorded almost 360 classical and other non-Christian authors quoted in his work.[204] Some of his arguments are found in the work of Justin Martyr, whom Clement had doubtless read.

The *Exhortation to the Heathen* was an evangelistic work to win pagans to Christ. The glory and purity of Christ is set out in contrast to the sordid licentiousness of paganism. It is a masterpiece of clarity and beauty in its composition, even though the orgies of the pagans are described in some detail. Clement did not spare the absurdity and cruelty of the pagan deities. Like Justin before him, he acknowledged that when both the high-minded philosophers and poets 'have given forth some utterances of truth, they bear indeed witness that the force of truth is not hidden, and at the same time expose their own weakness in not having arrived at the end.'[205]

The *Instructor* (or *Paedagogus*) in three books, is addressed to those who have turned from paganism; it is an encouragement to the development of Christian character and morality. The first book exhibits Christ as our great Instructor who is 'God in the form of man, stainless, the minister of His Father's will, the Word who is God, who is in the Father, who is at the Father's right hand, and with the form of God is God. He is to us a spotless image.'[206] The other two books in the *Instructor* set out rules for the Christian life. Clement listed the ways the Instructor uses to correct his children: admonition, upbraiding, complaint, invective, reproof, censure, denunciation, accusation and so forth! But always because he is the 'good Father'.

The instructions are detailed and practical, including eating and drinking: 'Some men, in truth, live that they may eat, as the irrational creatures, "whose life is their belly, and nothing else." But the Instructor enjoins us

204 So Stählin in Metzger, *The Canon of the New Testament*, p.131.
205 Clement of Alexandria, *The Exhortation*, Book I, Ch. 7.
206 Clement of Alexandria, *The Instructor*, Book I, Ch. 2.

to eat that we may live.'[207] Even laughter is included, and perfumes and jewellery, and 'sleeping' and the kind of bed that should be used: 'stretching one's self on even couches, affording a kind of natural gymnasium for sleep, contributes to the digestion of the food.' Clothes, shoes, with whom to associate, and much more, find their place in Clement's careful instructions. It may seem pernickety or even legalistic to us, but if we read first his pleading with the pagan to leave a wasteful and licentious life and follow Christ, we will understand where the young converts were coming from.

The *Miscellanies* (or *Stromata*), in eight books, sets out to defend the truth against the false teaching of the Gnostics. It presents a true Christian philosophy. The *Miscellanies* maintains that 'philosophy is the handmaid of theology'; in other words, it is merely a stepping stone towards the ultimate truth which is found only in Christ. But mere sophistry, a display of personal wisdom, is useless: 'To act well is far better than to speak well.'[208] Clement believed that there are fragments of truth in all systems, which may be separated from error; but that the truth can be only found in unity and completeness in Christ, since from him all the scattered gems originally came. In dealing with the Gnostics, Clement, with his massive store of knowledge from the philosophers and poets, demonstrated that the Gnostics are no more than Platonists in a new guise, and that true knowledge comes only from Christ.

Like Justin before him and Ignatius before that, Clement provided the church with strong arguments against both pagans and heretics, but there was no question of any of his writings being added to the list of apostolic books.

DIONYSIUS OF CORINTH

Dionysius is known to us only through the *Ecclesiastical History* of Eusebius. It is thought that he died around AD 170, but his birth date is unknown. This is the more surprising since he was an outstanding leader of the church in the second century and was bishop of Corinth at the time of

---

207 As above Book II, Ch.1.
208 Clement of Alexandria, *The Miscellanies*, Ch.10.

his death. He is remembered as a prolific writer of pastoral letters to various churches including Athens, Nicomedia, Lacedaemon, Crete and especially to Rome. Unfortunately, only fragments of his letters have survived although Eusebius offers a summary of seven letters from Dionysius.

ARISTIDES OF ATHENS

Little is known of Aristides, and only in 1878 was a copy of his *Apology* discovered in an Armenian translation and, in 1888 a version in Syriac also. However, it was widely circulated in its day and was referred to as late as the ninth century. Eusebius, in his *Ecclesiastical History*, records that it was sent to the emperor Hadrian and therefore can be dated around AD 126, whilst others believe it was intended for the Emperor Antoninus Pius which would date it after AD 138. Aristides demolished the gods of the 'Barbarians' who set up 'gods of earth, water, fire, wind, sun and even men.' He then turned his attention to the 'many fictitious gods' of the Greeks and then to the Egyptians 'because they are more base and stupid than every people that is on the earth.'[209] Finally there is a moving defence of the Christians and their life in fellowship with God and each other.

ATHENAGORAS OF ATHENS

Almost nothing is known about Athenagoras either, and his dates are equally uncertain. That he was a respected leader at Athens and wrote several works including *A Plea for the Christians*, are about the only indisputable facts. Fortunately, this work, written somewhere around AD 175, is available, and it reveals an able and courageous scholar. In it he defended the Christians against the charges that they were atheists, ate human flesh at the Lord's supper and committed incestuous sex: 'Three things are alleged against us: atheism, Thyestean feasts, Oedipodean intercourse. But if these charges are true, spare no class: proceed at once against our crimes; destroy us root and branch, with our wives and children, if any Christian is found to live like the brutes.'[210]

---

209 Aristides, *Apology*, Ch. 12.
210 Athenagoras, *A Plea for the Christians*, Ch. 3.

The writer showed himself well acquainted with the Greek and Roman poets and philosophers, including Thales, Plato and Socrates. He quotes them to defend the unity of God as One, and yet showed that the Christian doctrine is superior even to theirs. In a strong defence of the Trinity, Athenagoras declared that polytheism is absurd; there follows a thorough demolition of the myths of the gods and of their incestuous relationships. It is, he suggests 'nothing wonderful that they should get up tales about us such as they tell of their own gods.'[211]

By contrast, the high morality of the Christians is open for all to see, and their approach to marriage is a model for others to follow. Their firm belief in the resurrection may be absurd to their accusers, but it is hardly a crime.

The Emperor Marcus Aurelius was the recipient of this stout defence from the scurrilous attacks, and such a treatise must have put heart into the new converts who found themselves criticised for the very things that were abhorrent to them. The final plea to the Emperor is worth quoting and it speaks for itself as a testimony to the quiet, peaceable and law-abiding submission of the early Christians.

'And now do you, who are entirely in everything, by nature and by education, upright, and moderate, and benevolent, and worthy of your rule, now that I have disposed of the several accusations, and proved that we are pious, and gentle, and temperate in spirit, bend your royal head in approval? For who are more deserving to obtain the things they ask, than those who, like us, pray for your government, that you may, as is most equitable, receive the kingdom, son from father, and that your empire may receive increase and addition, all men becoming subject to your sway? And this is also for our advantage, that we may lead a peaceable and quiet life, and may ourselves readily perform all that is commanded us.'[212]

IRENAEUS OF LYONS
Born in the Roman province of Asia (modern Turkey) around AD 130, Irenaeus lived for seventy years and he ranks alongside Tertullian as one of the most exact and clear thinking theologians of the early church.

---

211 Athenagoras, *A Plea for the Christians*, Ch. 32.
212 As above, Ch. 37.

Irenaeus tells how he himself often listened to the elderly Polycarp, who was martyred for his faith in AD 155, relating his conversations with John. Irenaeus was therefore a 'grandson' of the apostles and, according to the later historian Eusebius, he recalled the detail of Polycarp's careful reflections on the life and ministry of Jesus as he himself had gained it from John: 'Things that Polycarp had heard directly from eyewitnesses of the Word of life and reported in full harmony with Scripture.'[213]

When Irenaeus moved to Rome, he came into contact with two of the leading Gnostic heretics of the day: Marcion and Valentinus. We do not know why he later migrated to Lyons, but he had arrived at a busy cosmopolitan river port with a population of some seventy thousand. Lyons was the provincial capital for Roman Gaul (France) and the centre for their transport system for the whole of the region. Christianity was well established here by the time Irenaeus arrived, but his passion for church planting meant that he learnt the local language. In his absence on one occasion, many Christians were martyred and he returned to a decimated and fearful church. Pothinus, at the age of ninety, was leader of the church and among those killed. Irenaeus was elected to take his place in AD 177.

Within five years he had begun his monumental (five volumes) written attack against the heretics. It is known to us as *Against Heresies* (*Adversus Haereses*), though it was known in his time as *A Refutation and Subversion of Knowledge Falsely So Called*. His original Greek version has come down to us only in a Latin translation. He wrote other works, but it is *Against Heresies* that we will refer to here, since it is a clear refutation of the views of Gnostics like Marcion and Valentinus—frequently quoting from their own work.

Until recently *Against Heresies* was a main source of information on the beliefs of the cults, however, with the discovery of the *Nag Hammadi Library* (see chapter 8), we now know how accurate Irenaeus was in relating their views. *Against Heresies* is much more than a refutation of error: it is also a clear statement of orthodox Christian truth.

---

213 Eusebius, *Ecclesiastical History*, Book V, Ch.19:5–7. Translated by Paul L Maier, *Eusebius: The Church History* (Kregel Publications, Grand Rapids 1999), p.195.

This eloquent leader at Lyons could rightly claim to represent the church across the empire and beyond; he insisted that the same message was preached by all the churches,[214] and therefore it was incumbent on the heretics to show that the universal church was in error. Irenaeus was aware of the subtleties of heretical teaching that made it so attractive to many:

'Error, indeed, is never set forth in its naked deformity, lest, being thus exposed, it should at once be detected. But it is craftily decked out in an attractive dress, so as, by its outward form, to make it appear to the inexperienced (ridiculous as the expression may seem) more true than the truth itself.'[215]

Those who today follow the fashionable trend of defending the Gnostics and their work as supposedly reliable and reflective of the second century church would do well to heed this warning.

Precisely how and when Irenaeus died is uncertain, though the year 200 is probably close, and some traditions claim that he died a martyr's death. His legacy was excellent.

It is clear from this brief survey, that the churches throughout the first one hundred years after the apostles, did not lack educated and courageous leaders who could defend the truth against heretics, Jews, pagan philosophers and even the Roman authorities. Their work reveals men with a sound knowledge of the classics and philosophers, the Old Testament Scriptures, and the writings of the apostles. Many of them breathe a warm pastoral heart, a clear academic mind, and a strong understanding of the true gospel. Yet not one of them was a candidate for inclusion into the canon of the New Testament. Beyond these, in the third and fourth centuries, men like Tertullian, Cyprian, Hippolytus, Origen and later still, Eusebius and Athenasius were able defenders of the faith against the growing influence of the Gnostics and others.

---

214 See chapter 1 under 'Why did it take so long?' Irenaeus, *Against Heresies*, Book I, Ch.10:2.
215 As above, Book I, Preface 2.

8. A library of lies

One of the most pressing influences that forced the early church to identify the books of the New Testament canon was the spread of deviant cults.

'Some mighty fiction'

False teachers, such as Marcion, Basilides, Montanus and Valentinus, challenged the mainstream teaching of the churches. They were supported by documents, letters and 'gospels', some claiming to come from the pen of the apostles themselves. In all, there are some sixty documents that make up what is known as the New Testament *pseudepigrapha*, a word meaning 'false writing'; the false gospels are often referred to as 'apocryphal gospels'. Even during the lifetime of Paul he warned the churches 'not to become easily unsettled or alarmed by some prophecy, report or letter supposed to have come from us' (2 Thessalonians 2:2).

Although much of the early false writing was influenced by the Gnostic heresy, they were not alone. The Montanists grew up in Phrygia in the middle of the second century and spread rapidly. An early form of extreme Pentecostalism, they practised ecstatic experiences of the Holy Spirit and were guided by revelations and prophecies given to Montanus. They produced their own 'scriptures' from these prophecies; Eusebius claimed an infinite number,[216] although none have so far survived. In addition, their emphasis on the end of the world and the extravagant language used, caused some of the churches to react against the Apocalypse of John and, because of the use the Montanists made of it, the epistle to the Hebrews also.

For their part, the Gnostics were not interested in doctrine or absolutes of theology, they preferred to express their religion in obscure statements and visionary insights. Irenaeus of Lyons, in his work *Against Heresies* was well acquainted with the false writings circulating in his day and he summarised the authors: 'Every one of them generates something new day

---

216 Eusebius, *Ecclesiastical History*, Book V, Ch. xvii.1. Eusebius exaggerated.

by day, according to his ability; for no one is deemed "perfect," who does not develop among them some mighty fiction.' [217] Irenaeus revealed their absurd interpretation of Scripture texts:

'But since they differ so widely among themselves both as respects doctrine and tradition, and since those of them who are recognized as being most modern make it their effort daily to invent some new opinion, and to bring out what no one ever before thought of, it is a difficult matter to describe all their opinions.' [218]

Significantly, the letters and 'gospels' of the *pseudepigrapha* served to confirm the churches in the truth of the Gospels and the letters of the apostles. The fact that they had a choice, and decisively rejected the *pseudepigrapha* speaks for itself. Far from challenging the canon of the New Testament, the *pseudepigrapha* actually confirmed it.

MARCION

Marcion, a wealthy ship-owner from Pontus on the Black Sea, arrived from Asia, where his extreme views had been rejected, and he made a generous donation to the church funds at Rome. Marcion believed passionately in Paul's doctrine of justification by faith, to the extent that he rejected the Old Testament altogether, believing it to be the product of an evil god, a demiurge. The old and new covenants were, according to Marcion, irreconcilable. He also believed that all the apostles had misunderstood Christ as the Jewish Messiah and therefore he accepted only Luke's Gospel and ten of Paul's letters; even these he severely edited, pruning Luke into what is possibly the *Gospel of the Lord*.[219]

In July AD 144, he was tried by the church at Rome, found guilty of heresy, and his monetary gift was handed back. The shipping magnate went off to spread his heresy elsewhere and started his own church. Tertullian wrote against Marcion,[220] and Justin Martyr, when writing his defence of the Christians to the Emperor Titus, tore into this arch heretic:

---

217 Irenaeus, *Against Heresies*, Book I, Ch.18:1.
218 *As above*, Book 1, Ch.21:5.
219 For an analysis of Marcion's editing see F F Bruce, *The Canon of Scripture*, pp.134–144.
220 Tertullian, *Against Marcion*, Book V.

'The devils put forward Marcion of Pontus, who is even now teaching men to deny that God is the maker of all things in heaven and on earth, and that the Christ predicted by the prophets is His Son, and preaches another god besides the Creator of all, and likewise another son.'[221]

Unfortunately, the edited canon of Marcion became widespread in the second century, especially in the West. But the fact that he could pick and choose from the books that were generally accepted, is clear evidence of a firming up of the canon prior to Marcion in the mid second century. Bruce concludes, '…it can be argued with some show of reason that Marcion's 'canon' was his revision of an existing collection of New Testament writings.'[222] And Metzger rightly claims, 'It is nearer to the truth to regard Marcion's canon as accelerating the process of fixing the Church's canon, a process that had already begun in the first half of the second century.'[223] Marcion may have the dubious honour of being the first to leave us a canon of New Testament books—an emasculated one.

THE GNOSTICS

Salvation for the Gnostics—scholars debate how much of a Gnostic Marcion was—became a matter of personal enlightenment or knowledge of the secret mysteries revealed in their own writings. *Gnosis* is a Greek word for knowledge. All Gnostics followed Marcion's dismissal of the Old Testament and its god, and believed that the natural, physical world was evil, because created by that evil demiurge; thus it was opposed to the spiritual world. This was a religious dualism that led them to despise the material life and encouraged some, like the followers of Carpocrates and his son Epiphanes, to practise some sordid rites. However, not all Gnostics used their beliefs as a licence for licentiousness, though all considered that salvation was through self-enlightenment and freeing oneself from the body which was the prison house of the soul.

The Gnostics believed that Jesus was the one to give this enlightenment, but their Jesus was very different from the Man portrayed in the four New

221 Justin Martyr, The first *Apology*, Ch. 58.
222 F F Bruce, *The Canon of Scripture*, p. 148.
223 Bruce Metzger, *The Canon of the New Testament* (Oxford University Press 1987), p. 99.

Testament Gospels. Most of them believed that the Christ only *seemed* to be a real man—a view known as Docetism from the Greek verb *dokein* 'to seem'—and that the Christ was substituted by another at the cross; some Gnostics believed it was Simon of Cyrene. This led to tales of Jesus visiting other lands, marrying Mary Magdalene and so forth.

Against Heresies by Irenaeus is a masterly demolition of the novelties of Gnosticism that reveals the author was thoroughly acquainted with the contemporary writings and well equipped to respond. He was not alone in asserting that the Gnostics could find no support for their views in the four Gospels, the Acts of the Apostles and the letters of Paul. Gnostics selected only the books they wanted from the New Testament, and claimed that the real message had been communicated secretly to the disciples (or some of them at least) and thus they could produce their own 'gospels' to reveal those secrets.

Irenaeus confirmed the widespread acceptance of the four canonical Gospels by showing how even the heretics used and abused them: 'So firm is the ground upon which these Gospels rest, that the very heretics themselves bear witness to them, and, starting from these, each one of them endeavours to establish his own peculiar doctrine.'[224] Tertullian complained in the same way: 'They actually treat of the Scriptures and recommend (their opinions) out of the Scriptures! To be sure they do. From what other source could they derive arguments concerning the things of the faith, except from the records of the faith?'[225]

Valentinus was another influential Gnostic leader, a native of Alexandria and contemporary of Marcion, who made use of *The Gospel of Truth* (see below). Valentinus often quoted from some of the books of the New Testament, though he twisted the texts with his own fanciful interpretations; a point which both Tertullian and Irenaeus were quick to recognise.[226]

Tertullian contrasted the methods of Marcion and Valentinus. Whereas Marcion used the knife to cut out passages he did not agree with, Valentinus simply twisted the meaning of Scripture to suit his own ends: 'He took

---

224 Irenaeus, *Against Heresies*, Book 3, Ch.11.7.
225 Tertullian, *The Prescription Against Heresies*, Ch.14.
226 Irenaeus, *Against Heresies*, Book 3, Ch.17:4.

away more, and added more, by removing the proper meaning of every particular word, and adding fantastic arrangements of things which have no real existence.' [227]

In addition to Marcion and Valentinus, Irenaeus singled out Basilides.[228] **Basilides** from Alexandria, perhaps the most able and certainly the most literary of the Gnostics, produced twenty-four books to expound Gnostic views; Irenaeus calls it 'an immense development to his doctrines.' [229] Only fragments of these remain today. Basilides presents an unholy mixture of Greek mythology and twisted gospel narrative which included the 'fact' that Simon of Cyrene was crucified in place of Jesus who, meanwhile, 'received the form of Simon, and, standing by, laughed at them.' [230]

Irenaeus also targeted **Carpocrates** who headed up a sect of Gnostics that believed Jesus was little more than any other man.[231] Clement of Alexandria hinted at their sordid nocturnal rites, whilst Irenaeus commented, 'They practise also magical arts and incantations; philtres [a drink to inflame the passions] and love-potions; and have recourse to familiar spirits, dream-sending demons, and other abominations.' [232]

Significantly, when Irenaeus condemned the Marcosians—another group of Gnostics from **Marcus**, a disciple of Valentinus—he specifically criticised them for inventing 'an unspeakable number of apocryphal and spurious writings, which they themselves have forged, to bewilder the minds of foolish men, and of such as are ignorant of the Scriptures of truth.' Irenaeus then referred to false statements, that we can now find in the *Gospel of Truth*.[233]

It is from these Gnostics that most of the false writings of the first few centuries came. Sadly, it was the Gnostic writings that influenced the first

227 As above, Ch. 38.
228 As above, Book 1, Ch. 14:3–7.
229 As above, Book 1, Ch. 24:3.
230 As above, Book 1, Ch. 24:4.
231 As above, Book 1, Ch. 25:1. 'They also hold that Jesus was the son of Joseph, and was just like other men, with the exception that he differed from them in this respect, that … he perfectly remembered those things which he had witnessed.'
232 As above.
233 As above, Book 1, Ch. 20:1.

understanding of the Christian Gospel by Mohammed early in the seventh century, and today the Qur'an perpetuates the long discredited stories of the Gnostics.[234]

There is evidence of around fourteen false gospels available today, though numbers will vary depending how the documents are classified. All were written much later than the apostles and four Gospels, and there is no evidence of any of them ever being considered for a place in the canon of the New Testament. All reveal Gnostic views, many are mere fragments—and some have been lost and we know them only by name. The following are a few that fairly represent the whole.

THE *GOSPEL OF JUDAS*—'A FICTITIOUS HISTORY'

The *Gospel of Judas* was launched into the world by the *National Geographic Magazine* in April 2006, with predictions that this revelation: 'could create a crisis of faith'. Others suggested that we may have to rethink the story of Christ in the light of this new revelation. All that is new about the fragmentary text is that for the first time in eighteen hundred years we can read it. The original was probably written just prior to AD 180 because in that year Irenaeus referred to a 'Gospel of Judas' in his treatise *Against Heresies*. Irenaeus summarised the *Gospel of Judas* accurately, and referred to it as 'a fictitious history ... which they style the Gospel of Judas'.[235]

This 'fictitious history' was discovered in Egypt in 1978. Written in Egyptian Coptic on thirteen pieces of papyrus, it took five years to reassemble, decipher and translate because of its poor condition; about fifteen percent has been irretrievably destroyed. The papyrus is a copy reliably dated between AD 220 and 340.

In brief, the *Gospel of Judas* tells the 'secret account of the revelation that Jesus spoke in conversation with Judas Iscariot during the week before he celebrated Passover.'[236] Only Judas could claim to know who

---

234 As an example, Mohammed claimed that Jesus did not die on the cross but only 'appeared to them like one crucified.' *Qur'an* ch.4, Al-Nisā, 158. See also under the *Infancy Gospel of Thomas* and the *Gospel of Philip* below.
235 Irenaeus, *Against Heresies*, Book 1, Ch.31:1.
236 The *Gospel of Judas*, ed. Kasser, Meyer and Wurst (The National Geographic Society 2006).

Jesus was, and he shared privately with Jesus that he had had a vision of all the disciples stoning him. In response, Jesus told him, 'But you will exceed all of them. For you will sacrifice the man that clothes me.' This reveals the Gnostic view that the Christ merely inhabited the body of a man (sometimes thought to be Simon of Cyrene) and left before the crucifixion. The esoteric (cryptic) language throughout is typical of all Gnostic writings. A reference to 'Sophia', the goddess of wisdom who was loved by the Gnostics, is included.[237]

THE *INFANCY GOSPEL OF THOMAS*

The earliest of the existing manuscripts for the *Infancy Gospel of Thomas* (not to be confused with the *Gospel of Thomas*, which is part of the *Nag Hammadi Library*, see below) is from the sixth century. The original may have been written in the middle of the second century. It fills the gap of the life of Christ up to the age of twelve. The book begins: 'The stories of Thomas the Israelite, the philosopher, concerning the works of the childhood of the Lord.'[238]

The writer includes a story that at the age of five Jesus fashioned twelve sparrows out of clay which, when he clapped his hands, they flew away.[239] It is followed by the account of a young lad who, having spoiled one of Jesus' miracles was punished by Jesus and he promptly 'withered up wholly.' Another lad bumped into him and was immediately struck dead. Others who admonished him, including his teachers, were struck with blindness or otherwise punished. The prodigious wisdom of Jesus amazed his teachers, and he could heal and even raise the dead. The account closes with the story of Jesus being left behind in Jerusalem, recorded in Luke 2:42–52.

---

237 Irenaeus refers to her cult more than thirty times and mocks the stupidity of Gnostic beliefs concerning her.

238 B H Cowper, *The Apocryphal Gospels and other Documents Relating to the History of Christ* (Williams and Norgate, London and Edinburgh, 1870), pp.128–169. All of these apocryphal books can be read on line by searching under their title, but quotations here are often from a nineteenth century volume to emphasise that there is nothing new in our knowledge of them.

239 The *Qur'an* refers to this account, ch. 5, Al-Māʾidah, 111. Mohammad could only have received this story from the *Infancy Gospel of Thomas* or the *Arabic Gospel of the Infancy*—both Gnostic books.

THE *ARABIC GOSPEL OF THE INFANCY*

Another attempt to add details to the silence of the four Gospels describes what happened when the family fled to Egypt. It is doubtful whether it was written much earlier than the eighth century, and clearly its intent was to exalt Mary who is the means of several miracles. The family even met the two thieves whom the Christ child prophesied would later be crucified with him. Having returned to Bethlehem, Jesus, at the age of seven made animals and birds of clay that then walk and fly. Here and there some phrases show acquaintance with the Gospels.

THE *GOSPEL OF PSEUDO MATTHEW*

Two documents are involved, both copies from the fifth century. The *Gospel of Pseudo Matthew* begins: 'The Book of the Birth of the Blessed Mary and of the Infancy of the Saviour. Written in Hebrew by the Blessed Evangelist Matthew, and translated into Latin by the Blessed Presbyter Jerome.'[240]

Mary is presented as a perfect child and her story begins at the age of three years. She received her food from the angels who talked often with her. Mary determined to remain a virgin all her life and eventually was committed to the care of Joseph, along with five other virgins. She becomes pregnant by the Holy Spirit and, with many embellishments, the story runs more or less parallel to the Gospels at this point. Significantly Luke 2:1–2 is quoted exactly but then the nativity is filled out with imaginary details. The story clearly reflects the widespread view in the fifth century of the perpetual virginity of Mary; a few miracles are added to prove it. The story continues through the circumcision of the child, the visit of the Magi, the slaughter of the boys in Bethlehem by Herod and the flight to Egypt. On the way, even lions and leopards adored him 'showing subjection by wagging their tails.' Various miracles follow including the idols of Egypt falling down. From here we are taken to the childhood of Jesus and some of the stories reflect those in the *Infancy Gospel of Thomas*.

It is clear that the writer was acquainted with the four Gospels, and at times can even quotes from them, although he never acknowledged his source.

---

240 B H Cowper, *The Apocryphal Gospels and other Documents Relating to the History of Christ*, pp. 29–83.

Chapter 8

THE *GOSPEL OF PETER*

This short and incomplete account was discovered in the Egyptian desert by a French archaeologist around 1886. It was a copy (possibly in the seventh to ninth centuries) of an original that may have been written in the middle of the second century. It begins with the trial of Jesus, and assumes that Herod was responsible for the crucifixion of Jesus. Joseph of Arimathea, 'the friend of Pilate', requested the body from the governor. The centurion given charge of the tomb is named as Petronius, and he pitched a tent for his men and kept guard, and saw bizarre visions of Jesus and the angels.

The story of Mary Magdalene and the women who came to the tomb follows fairly closely the Gospel records. Peter takes up the story from his own perspective, admitting that the disciples were all afraid and, without any reference to the appearances of Jesus in Jerusalem, concludes: 'But I, Simon Peter, and my brother Andrew, having taken our nets, went off to the sea. And there was with us Levi of Alphaeus whom the Lord...'[241]— and from here the rest is lost.

Among the *pseudepigrapha* are *The Preaching of Peter*, *The Acts of Peter*, *The Apocalypse of Peter*. None was accepted by the churches.

THE *HISTORY OF JOSEPH THE CARPENTER*

First published in 1722 it is thought to have originated in Coptic sometime in the fourth century, though some place it much later. Unlike other false writings, this one claims to have been related by Jesus himself. Referring to Mary he asserts: 'I loved her with a peculiar affection, with the good pleasure of my Father, and the counsel of the Holy Spirit; and I was incarnate of her, by a mystery surpassing the capacity of the reason of creatures.'[242] In addition to a few historical blunders, Joseph was widowed with a family before he married Mary who then bore the Christ as her only child. A large part of the account concerns the painful old age of Joseph until Christ gave him new health and he died at the age of one hundred and eleven years.

---

241 See Wesley Centre Online. Hosted by the Northwest Nazarene University, Idaho, 1993-2005, the *Gospel of Peter* XV.
242 Cowper, *The Apocryphal Gospels*, p.105.

THE *EPISTLE TO THE LAODICEANS*

The oldest copy known is dated AD 546, although it was mentioned by writers from the fourth century on. Pope Gregory the Great (AD 590–604), may have rescued it from oblivion, in which case he was especially gullible. Clearly Paul's reference in Colossians 4:16 was the cue for the anonymous forger who was little gifted either in counterfeit or a knowledge of the apostolic mind. It consists of a few scattered sayings culled from Paul's genuine letters, adds nothing new at all, makes no mention of anyone by name, and contains nothing to make it worthwhile the Colossians sending a messenger to Laodicea to collect a copy. It is found in not a single Greek text although it crept into many later Latin versions of the New Testament, including the Vulgate of Jerome in the fifth century.

Other *pseudepigrapha* provided letters written by Paul, Peter, Herod, Pilate, Joseph of Arimathea, the woman healed from an issue of blood (Matthew 9:20–22), and even by Jesus himself. We also have a little correspondence between Paul and Seneca, the Roman Philosopher and Nero's tutor!

The *Nag Hammadi Library*

In 1945, almost eighteen hundred years after Marcion was disciplined for heresy and Irenaeus had published his five volumes *Against Heresies*, an Arab peasant discovered a collection of old books close to Nag Hammadi, on the east bank of the Nile in Upper Egypt. It consisted of sixty-one fragments covering fifty-two separate documents in thirteen codices (books). They had been written sometime in the fifth century, although are probably copies from the third century. They are in Coptic, an old Egyptian language written mostly with Greek characters, and are now in the Coptic Museum in Old Cairo. For the most part we have only fragments or badly damaged copies. The Gnostics largely died out by the sixth century. The early church leaders who wrote against them are seen to have given an accurate assessment of Gnostic beliefs.

They are 'tedious and verbose',[243] and only a sample from Nag Hammadi can be given here. Irenaeus complained that: 'Every one of them

---

243 Bruce Metzger, *The Canon of the New Testament*, p. 77.

generates ... day by day ... some mighty fiction.'[244] The literature of the *Nag Hammadi Library* is part of that 'mighty fiction'.

THE *GOSPEL OF TRUTH*

The Gospel of Truth is the fullest expression of the Gnostic mind of all the books in the *Nag Hammadi Library,* and some believe that it is the work of the leading and influential Gnostic Valentinus, written around the middle of the second century. It reveals the Gnostic love of the obscure, and the theme is that ignorance of the Father is darkness and the darkness is dispelled only by attaining true knowledge of oneself and the world.

In a passage that reflects the 'monism' of Gnostic thinking we have the heart of Gnostic philosophy; monism is the denial of a distinction between matter and mind and a belief that all is One. The All appears frequently in Gnostic writing:

'Since the perfection of the All is in the Father, it is necessary for the All to ascend to him. Therefore, if one has knowledge, he gets what belongs to him and draws it to himself. For he who is ignorant, is deficient, and it is a great deficiency, since he lacks that which will make him perfect. Since the perfection of the All is in the Father, it is necessary for the All to ascend to him and for each one to get the things which are his. He registered them first, having prepared them to be given to those who came from him.'[245]

The *Gospel of Truth* bears no resemblance to the New Testament record of salvation, and presents a philosophy that cannot be considered as Christian spirituality. Irenaeus was aware of this so called 'gospel' since it had just begun circulating when it came to his attention.

'Indeed, they have arrived at such a pitch of audacity, as to entitle their comparatively recent writing *The Gospel of Truth*, though it agrees in nothing with the Gospels of the Apostles, so that they have really no Gospel which is not full of blasphemy...'[246]

---

244 Irenaeus, *Against Heresies*, Book I, ch.18.1.
245 Quotations from The Gnostic Society Library on line *The Gospel of Truth* from *Gnosticism.* (Harper & Brothers. New York 1961). Translated by Robert M. Grant.
246 *Against Heresies*, Book III, ch.11:9.

THE *GOSPEL OF THOMAS*

The *Gospel of Thomas* (not to be confused with the *Infancy Gospel of Thomas* described earlier) contains one hundred and fourteen sayings, supposedly of Jesus, revealed to the apostle Thomas. Many of these bear similarities with the teaching of Jesus. Some are straightforward quotations, which clearly reveals a knowledge of the Gospels. Thirteen parables are included that, though much shorter in Thomas, are paralleled in the Gospels. However, much else is vague and obscure:

'Jesus said to them, "When you make the two one, and when you make the inside like the outside and the outside like the inside, and the above like the below, and when you make the male and the female one and the same, so that the male not be male nor the female female; and when you fashion eyes in the place of an eye, and a hand in place of a hand, and a foot in place of a foot, and a likeness in place of a likeness; then will you enter the kingdom"' (22).[247]

It has been claimed by some that one reason why the Gnostic gospels were destroyed was because they revealed the 'true' story of the leadership of women in the first century church. If this is so, what should we make of this:

'Simon Peter said to them, "Let Mary leave us, for women are not worthy of Life." Jesus said, '"I myself shall lead her in order to make her male, so that she too may become a living spirit resembling you males. For every woman who will make herself male will enter the Kingdom of Heaven"'? (114).

Irenaeus made no direct reference to the *Gospel of Thomas*, and since he was familiar with most of the Gnostic writings, it suggests that this one had not been written before AD 180.

THE *GOSPEL OF PHILIP*

The *Gospel of Philip* does not claim to be the teaching of Jesus, but is a handbook of Gnostic thinking. Much of it is obscure. For example:

247 Quotations from the *Gospel of Thomas* from The Gnostic Society Library on line. James M Robinson. ed. The *Nag Hammadi Library*. Revised edition (HarperCollins, San Francisco, 1990). Translated by Thomas O Lambdin.

'Light and Darkness, life and death, right and left, are brothers of one another. They are inseparable. Because of this neither are the good good, nor evil evil, nor is life life, nor death death. For this reason each one will dissolve into its earliest origin. But those who are exalted above the world are indissoluble, eternal.' [248]

Some of the expressions are heretical, for which the early church leaders rightly condemned them. Here, the Virgin Birth is denied:

'Some said, "Mary conceived by the Holy Spirit." They are in error. They do not know what they are saying. When did a woman ever conceive by a woman? ... And the Lord would not have said, "My Heavenly Father" unless he had had another father, but he would have said simply "My Father".' [249]

According to this 'gospel', the world came about through a mistake: 'For he who created it wanted to create it imperishable and immortal. He fell short of attaining his desire. For the world never was imperishable, nor, for that matter, was he who made the world.' [250]

Wildly extravagant claims are made suggesting that the *Gospel of Philip* reveals that Jesus and Mary were married. In fact, there is not one word or phrase in any literature of the first four centuries that makes this claim.

THE *GOSPEL OF MARY* [MAGDALENE]

Much of this has been lost and it is hardly possible to assess what Mary really said because large sections are missing. What we have is the mystic teaching attributed to Mary Magdalene. After the ascension of Christ, the disciples were in despair and it is Mary who rouses them to action and courage:

'Then Mary stood up, greeted them all, and said to her brethren, "Do not weep and do not grieve nor be irresolute, for His grace will be entirely with you and will protect you. But rather, let us praise His greatness, for He has prepared us and made us into

---

248 Quotations from The Gnostic Society Library on line. James M Robinson ed. The *Nag Hammadi Library*. Translated by Wesley W. Isenberg.
249 The repeated denials in the *Qur'an* of the virgin conception and Jesus as the Son of God show the influence of Gnostic teaching on Mohammed's understanding of the Christian faith, eg. *Qur'an*, Ch 6, Al-an'ām, 102; Ch 10, Yūnus, 69; Ch 19, Maryam, 92–93.
250 As above, The *Gospel of Philip*. Translated by Wesley W Isenberg.

Men." When Mary said this, she turned their hearts to the Good, and they began to discuss the words of the Saviour. Peter said to Mary, "Sister we know that the Saviour loved you more than the rest of women. Tell us the words of the Saviour which you remember which you know, but we do not, nor have we heard them." Mary answered and said, "What is hidden from you I will proclaim to you."'[251]

The book reveals Mary Magdalene as a favourite of Jesus and one who possessed a knowledge and spirituality superior to that of the Apostles. Nothing more is written about her relationship to Jesus than this.

THE *GOSPEL OF THE EGYPTIANS*

This is the most bizarre of all the documents in the Hammadi Library. Some of the early church leaders were aware of it, but all rejected it entirely as spurious. Large sections are missing and it gives the impression of the ramblings of a deranged mind.

Written by 'Eugnostos the beloved' (whoever he was), it claims to be 'The Holy Book of the Great Invisible Spirit', and is full of symbol and unintelligible language. Three specimens, typical of the entire document, will suffice.

'Three powers came forth from him; they are the Father, the Mother, (and) the Son, from the living silence, what came forth from the incorruptible Father. These came forth from the silence of the unknown Father.'[252]

Later, the name of the 'Father of Light' is offered in the weird formulae of seven vowels each reproduced twenty-two times:

'Domedon Doxomedon came forth, the aeon of the aeons, and the throne which is in him, and the powers which surround him, the glories and the incorruptions ... he whose name is in an invisible symbol. A hidden, invisible mystery came forth: iiiiiiiiiiiiiiiiiiiii EEEEEEEEEEEEEEEEEEEEEE oooooooooooooooooooooo uuuuuuuuuuuuuuuuuuuuuu eeeeeeeeeeeeeeeeeeeeee aaaaaaaaaaaaaaaaaaaaaa OOOOOOOOOOOOOOOOOOOOOO'

---

251 As above, the *Gospel of Mary*. Translated by George W Macrae and R Mc L Wilson.
252 As above, the *Gospel of the Egyptians*. Translated by Alexander Bohlig and Frederik Wisse.

The theology of the Logos similarly defies clarity:

'The great Logos, the divine Autogenes, and the incorruptible man Adamas gave praise, (and) they asked for a power and eternal strength for the Autogenes, for the completion of the four aeons … the incorruptible man Adamas asked for them a son out of himself, in order that he (the son) may become father of the immovable, incorruptible race, so that, through it (the race), the silence and the voice may appear, and, through it, the dead aeon may raise itself, so that it may dissolve.'

The *Gospel of the Egyptians* is an extreme example, but it was significant enough for the Gnostics to add it to the collection at Nag Hammadi.

THE *APOCRYPHON OF JAMES*

These are secret revelations to James (the brother of Jesus) and to Peter. It is in the form of a conversation between Jesus and his disciples and, apparently, these are things that Jesus 'did not wish to tell to all of us, his twelve disciples.' We may question whether Jesus would ever have said, either openly or in secret: 'The Father has no need of me, for a father does not need a son, but it is the son who needs the father, though I go to him. For the Father of the Son has no need of you.'[253]

'Falsely called knowledge'

The Gnostics had been on the fringe early in the life of the churches. It is likely that some of the letters of the apostles were intended to undermine their deviant doctrine. Paul warned Timothy about 'opposing ideas of what is falsely called knowledge' (1 Timothy 6:20), and similarly set the Colossians on their guard against 'hollow and deceptive philosophy' and those whose 'unspiritual mind puffs him up with idle notions' (Colossians 2:8,18). When Paul prayed that the Colossians might: 'be filled with a knowledge of his will, through all spiritual wisdom and understanding', he was perhaps deliberately using the very words so central to Gnostic philosophy: *knowledge, wisdom, understanding*. John laid emphasis upon the true light and truth and testing the spirits (1 John

---

253 As above, the *Apocryphon of James*. Translated by Francis E Williams.

1:5–7; 4:1–3). Similarly, the errors denounced by Peter and James fit the beliefs of the Ophites, a sect of the Gnostics known also as Cainites; according to Irenaeus of Lyons, the false *Gospel of Judas* came from this stable.[254] Bishop Ellicott commented in the nineteenth century: 'They are weak, silly and profitless … they are despicable monuments even of religious fiction.'[255]

The Middle Ages saw a revival of interest in the apocryphal documents and some were useful to bolster the errors of the Roman Church. The *History of Joseph the Carpenter* supports the doctrine of the perpetual virginity of Christ. Many of the apocryphal stories found their way into the Morality and Miracle plays that were so popular in the Middle Ages, and into art, the Breviary, and later into our Christmas carols as well—the ox and the ass adoring the infant Christ is found in the *Gospel of Pseudo-Matthew*.[256]

Against all reason and good scholarship, in recent years some have suggested that in these documents we have the original gospels and beliefs of the early church. However, even taken all together, we could not make a coherent record of the life and teaching of Christ equal to any one of the four Gospels. The Gnostic writings bear no comparison with the simple and straightforward teaching of the four, nor were they meant to, because only the enlightened could gain salvation through the knowledge of the mysteries.

No one should read the *pseudepigrapha* without reading the four Gospels. Only then, as Metzger comments, 'One can appreciate the character of the canonical Gospels and the near banality of most of the gospels dating from the second and third centuries.'[257]

---

254 Irenaeus, *Against Heresies*, Book I, Ch. 31:1.
255 Bishop Ellicott, *Cambridge Essays* 1856, p.157. Quoted in Cowper, *The Apocryphal Gospels*, p.xlvii.
256 A useful survey of this subject in Cowper, *The Apocryphal Gospels*, Introduction pp. xxviii–xlvii and p.53.
257 Bruce Metzger, *The Canon of the New Testament*, p.173.

Appendix

The following chart can be downloaded as a PDF.
Go to https://www.dayone.co.uk/collections/books/all-you-need-to-know

Church Fathers, unknown authors and heretics

Note that this is not a complete list but those church leaders, unknown writers and heretics who are referred to in this book. The dates in most cases are approximate and may differ by a few years in various authorities.

Name	City of leadership	Dates (m=martyred)	Chief work	Contribution to the idea of a canon
Clement	Rome (Italy)	c.95	Letter to the Corinthians.	Quoted from or referred to more than half NT books and believed Paul wrote 'in the Spirit' and were 'Scriptures'.
Ignatius	Antioch (Syria)	50–115m	Seven letters on his way to martyrdom.	Widely alluded to most of NT and used only these for his authority. They were 'the ordinances of the Lord and of the Apostles.'
Polycarp	Smyrna (Asia)	70–155m	Letter to the Philippians.	Quoted from 16 NT books, and no others, to challenge the church. Referred to them as 'Sacred Scriptures.'
Papias	Hierapolis (Phrygia)	69–135m	Testimony to the authorship of Mark and Matthew.	Clearly familiar with John's Gospel, 1 Peter, 1 John and Revelation. Also had access to oral teachings.
The Didache		c.50–80	Author unknown. Practical Christian teaching.	The author knew and quoted from Matthew but of little value in determining what was accepted.
Epistle of Barnabas		c.130	Author unknown. Against Judaisers in the church.	He quotes from the NT but is of little value in determining what was accepted.
The Shepherd of Hermas	Rome	c.150	The author Hermas is unknown. Visions, commandments and parables.	Of little value in determining what was accepted.
The Muratorian Canon	Rome?	150–200	Author unknown. The oldest known list of NT books.	The complete NT with the exception of 1 and 2 Peter, James and Hebrews.

Name	Location	Date	Works	Description
Justin	Rome	100–165m	Two *Apologia* and a *Dialogue with Trypho* the Jew.	Defended the apostolic authority of the Four Gospels. Introduced quotations by 'it is written'.
Dionysius	Corinth (Greece)	??–170	Many pastoral letters to the churches. Only small fragments remain.	He contrasts his own letters with 'the Scriptures (writings) of the Lord.'
Tatian	Rome	110–180	Harmony of the Four Gospels (*Diatessaron*). *An Address to the Greeks*.	Only the Four Gospels accepted by the churches.
Aristides	Athens (Greece)	Writing c.126	An *Apology* to Emperor Hadrian	No reference from Scripture but to the Gospel and Christian 'books'.
Athenagoras	Athens	Writing c.175	*A Plea for the Christians* and *On the Resurrection of the Dead*	A few quotations from the Gospels and the epistles, but more would not be appropriate since his work is addressed to the emperor.
Irenaeus	Lugdunum (Lyons)	130–202	*Against Heresies* and defended the four Gospels.	Quoted over 1,000 passages from all but four or five NT books. They are 'the Scriptures' given by the Holy Spirit.
The Scilitan Martyrs	Carthage (N. Africa)	180m	On trial before proconsul Saturninus.	The epistles of Paul circulating in Latin in North Africa by AD 180. Almost certainly also the Four Gospels.
Tertullian	Carthage	155–220	*Apologeticus*: defence of the Christian faith *Spectaculis*: theology and against heretics.	The first serious expositor and used almost all the NT books. They were equated with OT and he referred to 'the majesty of our Scriptures.' He clearly possessed a canon almost, if not wholly, identical to ours,
Cyprian	Carthage	210–258m	*The Unity of the Church* and many letters.	Quoted from almost ten percent of NT and as 'Scripture'.
Hippolytus	Rome	170–235m	Forty works including commentaries and Christian doctrine.	Used much of the NT and as 'Scripture'. Quoted from other books but not with the same authority.
Clement	Alexandria (Egypt)	153–216	*Exhortation to the Heathen*. *The Instructor*. *The Miscellanies*.	Quoted from all but five NT books more than 3,000 time and believed them to be 'Scripture'. No other books given the same authority.

Name		Dates	Chief work	
Origen	Alexandria	180–253	Great biblical scholar. Expounded almost all books of the Bible. Referred to the 'New Testament'.	By AD 240 he listed the 27 books of our canon as 'Scripture'.
Eusebius	Caesarea (Judaea)	260–340	*Ecclesiastical History*—the 'Father of Church History'.	Listed 22 books as unquestioned by any church. The other five (James, Jude, 2 Peter and 2 and 3 John) were widely used among the churches.
Athanasius	Alexandria	296–373	A strong defender of the truth against Arius who denied the deity of Christ. He also distinguished between heretical book and useful (though not canonical) books.	Athanasius provides the oldest list of NT books identical with our 27: 'Let no one add to them, nor take anything from them' (AD 367).
Augustine	Hippo (N Africa)	354–430	*Confessions; Letters* and *The City of God*.	The Council of Hippo AD 393. For the NT only the 27 books.
Jerome	Rome & Antioch etc	347–420	Commentaries and the complete Bible in Latin: the *Vulgate*.	His NT canon only the 27, though accepted the selected books of the *Apocrypha*.

Some heretics

Name	City of leadership	Dates	Chief work	Chief heresy
Marcion	Rome and elsewhere	85–160	Only one book *Antisthenes* (Contradictions). But one of the earliest exponents of Gnostic views.	Gnosticism. Rejection of entire Old Testament and selection of a few New Testament books.
Montanus	Asia	?		Montanism. a form of extreme pentecostalism.
Valentinus	Egypt and Rome	100–160	Opened an influential school in Rome.	Gnosticism.
Marcus	Disciple of Valentinus	?	Leader of the Morcosians.	Gnosticism.
Basilides	Alexandria	117–138	Twenty-four books of *Exegetica*. Only fragments remain.	Gnosticism.
Carpocrates	Alexandria	?	Founded a Gnostic sect.	Practised magic and spiritism.

Index to significant subjects

These references will take the reader only to the book and chapter (eg 1/3, 4/5) in this series where the more significant references to the subject occur.

Index to significant subjects

Index to significant subjects

Index to main Scripture references

These references will take the reader only to the book and chapter (eg 1/3, 4/5) in this series where the more significant Scripture references occur.